Faithful?

Foolish?

Called

Recognising God's call
And what to do about it

Mark Tanner

LITTLE HOUSE IN
- JOPPA -

Little House in Joppa Publishing
Abbey Street, Chester, CH1 2JD, UK

admin@little-house-in-joppa.uk

First edition: 2023

ISBN: 978-1-7392688-6-2

DEDICATION

For the deacons and all who serve:

Your generosity, care, and service is more valued
than you will ever know.

Take good care to observe the commandment and instruction
that Moses the servant of the Lord commanded you, to love the
Lord your God, to walk in all his ways, to keep his
commandments, and to hold fast to him, and to serve him with
all your heart and with all your soul.' (Joshua 22.5)

INDEX

FOREWORD

_____

Whatever your reason for reading this book, you'll find here an invitation to spend time with God by spending time with others. First of all, Bishop Mark himself. Mark brings all his experience as vicar, bishop, military chaplain, Warden of Cranmer Hall to the pages of this book. But he draws, too, on the wisdom of those who have journeyed with him, sharing some of their stories as well as his own.

Some of 'the others' you will be with in this book are those whose lives and testimonies we find in the pages of scripture and also the spirit filled writers of scripture themselves. You will find examples of foolishness and faithfulness. You will find people who got it wrong as well as people who tried to get it right. You will find people like you, and people you aspire to be.

All this is a powerful reminder that none of us is called in isolation – we are called to be with each other, but most importantly we are called to be with God in Christ. In this we should find joy and hope. It is his ministry, not ours.

Vocation is about ordering our whole life towards God. But we are called to do this in community - with each other. In this vocation those things which shape our Christian life, the disciplines of prayer, reading Scripture, listening for God's voice, joining in God's mission in the world are both the means by which vocation grows and the end to which vocation reaches. We are called to participate with God in God's mission of love to the world. We all have a part to play. We are all called to work out what that means.

Hopefully you've picked up this book because God is already nudging you in a certain direction. Perhaps it is because you are wondering 'what next'.

God calls all of us. Not just those who do it 'professionally' and wear a collar – deacons, priests, and bishops. Yes, there are those who are set apart for a specific ministry, but each one of us has a vocation. It is part of our baptismal identity, that is, it is part of what it means to be raised with Christ to a new life, and what it means to be part of his Body, the Church, where each member is precious and valuable.

This book calls us to attend to God; to attend to those with whom we share our life; and to attend to ourselves. It is far more than a simple discussion of vocation, but rather an invitation into living the life each of us is called to, as created in the image of God and a member of God's Church.

I hope that as you spend time with this book, you enjoy the words and their invitation as much as Bishop Mark has enjoyed writing them. Be encouraged by his wisdom, grace, humility, and humour. And reach out in service to the God who has reached out to you in Christ.

God is calling you. It matters. Here's a book to find out why and how.

+Stephen Ebor

PREFACE TO THE FIRST EDITION

Two of my greatest privileges in life are opening the Bible with people and standing back amazed as they step into the stuff that God is calling them to do and to be.

This book is a seriously playful attempt to offer both of these gifts in written form. It is meant to be enjoyed. It is intended to provoke. It offers questions, and insights, and breathing spaces. It tries to curate a space where you can engage with God and his deep invitations to you.

My prayer is that, in reading this and wrestling with the various topics we explore, you will find you faith deepened, your understanding enlarged, and your heart warmed... and that you will hear and understand just a bit more of God's call on your life. Where he calls, he will also equip.

This book is offered with a deliberately improvised and playful feel. Vocation always seems to feel a bit 'rough and ready' when it is ours (and looks very polished in others), and

I want to reflect this. So, there might be some typos, for which I apologise (you are welcome to point them out if you wish, sending them to corrections@little-house-in-joppa.uk with book title, format, and page number). What I really hope, though, is that you can eavesdrop on a living set of conversations about vocation and join in: you can be part of this story too.

God bless you as you enter this exploratory space.

† Mark
April 2023

INTRODUCTION

What is God asking you to do with your life?

Might he have something specific in mind?

Are your restless in your Spirit and looking for something that will make a difference?

How would you know if God were calling?

Does Christ only call 'holy' people?

These, and countless questions like them, are exciting, urgent, and real questions. The fact that you have picked this book up probably means you are asking some of them and that is great... like really GREAT! God loves to engage with this kind of question, and this book is designed to help. Here you will meet a whole load of people wrestling with the same sort of questions, and a couple of big characters from the Bible who ought to have been wrestling with it. We will have a bit of fun as we reflect on a chunk of the Bible, and learn positive and negative lessons about 'vocation' (which is simply a posh word for God calling us to do stuff).

First, though, let's pray, and then I'll introduce the book a bit more formally.

Loving God,
Open our hearts again to one another,
to Your Spirit, and to Your Word, we pray,
That we might continue to be formed in Your image,
Released in Your service,
And share in the joy of knowing ourselves
to be utterly Yours,
For we ask in Your name, Amen.

Before we go any further, let me say that when I say 'vocation' I am talking about Christ-shaped vocation, but I don't only mean ministerial vocation and I certainly don't mean to confine my thoughts to the Church of England (although I recognise that I am located in both of those contexts). This text ends with some others' reflections on their own vocation (and there will be more online), and these are deliberately drawn from a variety of contexts. They are a snapshot of what I am talking about: none is complete, but all are beautiful and a gift to be received. You won't find an exact mirror of yourself in these pages, but I pray you will meet Jesus and hear his unique call afresh, whether for the first or the fiftieth time.

I'm grateful to a lot of people who got me thinking about this material. These reflections are mine, but they are a bit like vocation itself in one way: they are personal, but have also been shaped, enabled, released, and enriched by many others. The thinking was encouraged by a couple of colleagues who challenged me to develop a sermon I preached last year and left me living in a particular chunk of 1 Kings. It has been stretched by other friends and colleagues whom you will glimpse in this text, and it has been lived in my working context of Chester Diocese. The pondering behind this work is shared, the book itself is now shared, the fruit of it will (I hope) be shared: vocation is a shared work.

As I said to the Deacons being ordained here last year:

> ... we need to be really cautious about anything in ministry that comes just from us. You are about to be ordained Deacon.
>
> You know that 'Deacon' means to serve.
>
> By definition, you cannot do that just by yourself; even if you are the only one serving you still need someone to serve, and in truth most excellent service requires teamwork. There is almost nothing in ministry that you can do by yourself. It is a corporate thing. We are enablers of the body of Christ. We are part of that body and therefore the fact that these thoughts come not just

*from me seems to me a really important part of the gift
that we receive this afternoon.*

Just as others have enabled me to bring this reflection to
light, so each of us needs to take it forward for ourselves if it
was to be useful. This book is not finished work, either in the
sense of having mined the full riches of the passages we will
consider, or the actual inhabiting of the vocations we are
discussing. I joked with the Deacons about setting them the
homework of completing my thinking, of living for
themselves in the chapters we would be considering in order
to reflect on their own vocation. I have no idea how many of
them did so, but you who read this book face the same
challenge. Vocation is not theoretical. Vocation is not
something I can describe, inhabit, or understand in isolation.
Rather it is Christ's call shared with his whole church,
sometimes working through us as individuals. It is ours not
mine, offered not earned, shared not possessed, and it
primarily concerns service not reward. It dances to the
rhythms of love, freedom, grace, joy, hope, and beauty, and
marches to the drumbeats of obedience, discipline,
sacrifice, duty, and even crucifixion. This is the LORD's work
in which we participate and into which we are called.

All of which means that our vocation is one of the toughest
and most precious things we will ever engage with, and at
the same time, it is something we must hold lightly and
patiently. Vocation is rarely rushed and is usually crushed if
it becomes overly intense. Andy, my chaplain, observed that

he thinks Ahab and Jezebel are a bit like the Panto[1] section of the Old Testament. Jezebel appears and we are meant to shout 'she's behind you' or give ourselves over to a bit of a 'boo' and an overly dramatic 'hiss'. I love this insight! The thought stuck: you will see it developed and, even though the text is clearly more than simply a pantomime, I hope that you read this with a smile on your face.

For the 'panto' chapters (which comment on the biblical text), you would probably do well to read with a Bible alongside you so that you are not just reading my version of the events. I have tried not to assume too much familiarity with the stories, but neither have I completely retold them. Moreover, you will notice things from 1 Kings that I have not picked up, and these will probably be far more important in your journey, your enjoyment, and your engaging in what God is saying than my 'take' on the story. Both the Bible and pantomime are best enjoyed first-hand.

The book is structured around an extended reflection on 1 Kings 17-22, interspersed with some reflections on vocation, some negative lessons from the text, some positives, and an exploration of what I notice about vocation today. At the end of the book you will find some reflections on how you might discern vocation in yourself and others, if that is what

---

[1] 'Panto' or pantomime is a light-hearted, largely British, form of theatre which has lots of slapstick humour and is intended for the whole family. It has a stylised and robust way of naming evil and mocking it safely whilst communicating morals in such a trite manner that it gets past our defences.

you are looking for. I have spread out the biblical material throughout the book, so depending on your reading style and what you are focussing your reflections on, there are (at least) two ways you could read this book.

1)   You might like to start at the beginning and work through. This will be like going to the theatre with friends, and coming in and out of the story whilst you talk about the things that matter in between. Even if you do this, you could read the whole 1 Kings 17-22 before you start to get an overview of the events we are considering.

2)   Maybe, though, you want to explore the whole biblical text in one chunk (I think that might be my preferred way of reading it if it were me, so don't feel you shouldn't do this). The chapters are clearly titled, and the biblical material is on different coloured pages to enable this. This way of reading would immerse you in the biblical narrative as a whole before engaging in wider reflections on vocation. The chapter order, should you choose this route, would be Introduction, 1, 2, 4, 5, 7, 8, 10, 3, 6, 9, 11.

Whichever way you choose to read, please keep your Bible handy! My reading of the text is not a replacement for the text itself.

Please remember that I am expressing my own views not making a formal statement for the Church of England.

Finally, do notice that there is a lot of pressure which makes us to take this work, and even ourselves, dreadfully seriously. In many ways we should, of course, but it is the LORD we really take seriously: I know I am merely a man of unbridled idiocy living among a people of only marginally more bridled foolishness, this is how it is, how it always has been, and how I suspect it always will be. As it was for Elijah, Obadiah, Elisha, and Micaiah, so it is for me and for you: it is the call of God that means we are sent, not our own marvelousness. Vocation doesn't make me a superhero; it simply hitches me onto the shoulders of the One who is really in charge. I invite you to inhabit a small portion of the Hebrew Scriptures with me as we reflect on the nature and substance of vocation as we are called to it today in serving our nation and the LORD's church...

... and please enjoy it (not every word of this book should be taken seriously) for in so doing you might join Lucy, Susan, Peter, and Edmund (from the Narnia books) and see right through this boxy little wardrobe into the woods beyond...

So come with me to 1 Kings 16.

1. THE DRAMA BEGINS:
INTRODUCTION AND INTRODUCTIONS

The scene is set... the warm-up acts have scampered on and off the stage in 1 Kings 16, and now the main drama begins. We are about to meet Ahab, Jezebel, and a variety of prophets in a focussed and concise 'chunk' of Hebrew history which misses out far more than it includes.

On this stage there will be no reflection of the political savvy of the new King of a weak kingdom marrying the daughter of a powerful neighbour... rather we are presented with the mocking antithesis of a pantomime dame that is King Ahab stumbling onto the stage with all of the foolishness of the dame but none of the harmless goodness.

Here is the evil witch, the dark sister, the original Jezebel (boo, hiss... she's behind you) made darker and infinitely more stereotyped by the medieval misogyny and racism of the church and wider society, but still an archetypal baddy.

Here is a succession of prophets starting with Elijah and ending with Micaiah having met Elisha and a number of unnamed prophets en route. Each has their part: the hero, the coward, the poet, the comedian, to name but a few aspects of their rich and complex roles.

This is partly pantomime but it is so much more besides. It is partly light-hearted morality play, but is far more insightful and is often painfully funny. It's serious stuff held lightly. It concerns kingship and prophecy, and in the Hebrew Scriptures this means it is about vocation. Three groups of people were set apart by anointing in what we call the Old Testament: prophets, priests, and kings. Each in their own way share part of God's work by his invitation (and calling, hence 'vocation' from the Latin 'vocare', to call).

Let's turn our mind, then, to the text, to this panto that is more than simply pantomime, to the drama into which we are invited, namely 1 Kings 16.29 through to 1 Kings 22.40, the story of Ahab, Jezebel, and the prophets of the living God.

Introductions (1 Kings 16.29-17.1)

Ahab appears on the 1 Kings stage at chapter 16, verse 29, and it really isn't a very promising start. There's a bum-note from the chorus, a deliberately mis-placed prop, and the son of Omri stumbles into the limelight. We are right in the middle of the tangled list of kings of Judah and Israel: if you're anything like me, you get dreadfully confused about which kingdom is which, and which king comes where and so on and so forth, but listen up! 'Ahab, son of Omri reigned over Israel in Samaria for 22 years and did evil in the sight of the LORD more than all who were before him'.

Clang. Left foot in bucket, and here comes the right one into another: 'as if it had been a light thing for him to walk in the sins of Jeroboam son of Nebat, he took as his wife Jezebel daughter of King Ethbaal of the Sidonians and went and served Baal and worshipped him'.

It's not a promising start, but there is another character (or group of characters, really) who will guide our attention for the next six chapters, and we meet him at the start of Chapter 17: enter Elijah who is well known from other parts of the Bible but enters 1 Kings at this point. On he comes, walks straight up to the King and without a 'by your leave' says 'As the LORD the God of Israel lives, before whom I stand, there shall be neither dew nor rain these years, except by my word.'

Interestingly we are not told that Elijah is a prophet before he speaks, although verse 2 of chapter 17 does let us know that the word of the LORD comes to him (as it will do on a number of occasions in the coming verses). The scene is set. The bad king, the non-believing wife, and the confrontational prophet.

Relax and enjoy these five chapters! Don't rush them. Don't try to control them. Open yourself to let them do their own work in you. and ask yourself the really simple repeated question. What does this teach me about Godly vocation? Allow yourself to notice what you are being taught to avoid, or to seek, or to practise, or to learn. Where should you hang around, and when should you flee?

My basic thesis here is that these chapters are largely a kind of midrash[2] on Godly vocation: a chunk of Jewish discursive teaching which deliberately meanders around a serious and complex subject in order to draw us towards understanding and the inhabiting of wisdom. This is one of the ways the Bible and the people of God explore wisdom, I think. (They are not technically a midrash, of course, not least because they are directly in

---

[2] 'Midrash' is a Jewish form of teaching which discusses the biblical text and which seems to me often to do so by embracing new or extended stories. Jewish teachers are often able to hold the text more lightly than we Christians are, and in so doing delve more robustly into their depths. This is what we are trying to do here.

the scriptures, but they embody the more expansive, discursive, inquisitive, reflective, and indeed Jewish teaching style of the midrashim.) Here I describe it as 'panto' because we are familiar with that concept (there are more formal terms I would use elsewhere): we should not despise the place of humour in the exploration of wisdom, vocation, and identity. These chapters reflect profoundly and explicitly on the nature of Godly kingship and, in so doing, also reflect on the place of the prophet. The king fails, the prophets challenge but do so in a manner which is personal, costly, and creative.

Here, in a six-act drama, we will glimpse some of the characteristic failures of vocations and some of the things that feed it. With care we will notice the kind of things that God looks for, calls out, and enables. However, it might be worth reminding ourselves of what happens in the text before reflecting further. Please let me encourage you to have your Bible open as you read the rest of this chapter. We shall be zipping through the text pausing only to draw out pertinent details and highlight the flow of the narrative.

2. PANTO ACT 1:
ELIJAH AND GOD'S PROVISION
(1 KINGS 17)

Are you sitting comfortably?

Right, we've met the characters, let's get on with the show. Act One is ready to start and one of the main characters is about to appear. Here comes Elijah who has just prophesied drought and promises much. Conflict? Violence? Clever speeches? Hush, and listen!

Scene 1 (vv2-7)

Elijah, the hero is sent by God...

.... to the Wadi Cherith where water will continue to flow despite the drought, and he is fed by ravens. He duly obeys, goes, and is both fed and watered until the wadi dries up. A wadi is a valley where a stream flows in the rainy season, which means the drying is no great surprise, although we are not actually told how long he was there. Being fed by ravens, especially being fed with bread they are quite fond of eating for themselves, though, definitely falls into miraculous territory. The detail, though, is not the concern of the passage. This story, like Elijah's diet, is simple rations.

What may be more surprising, at least to the discerning reader (for, like panto, this is a drama that works on many levels concurrently) is the two-fold 'Cherith' and 'ravens'. 'Cherith' means 'cut-off', 'excommunicated', or 'divorced'. Ravens are unclean according to Jewish law, although he does not eat the ravens, of course. The nonsense in this text is not just a human attempt to be funny or engaging, it is divine in the very best sense: God is at the heart of the mystery. The prophet who will bring God's message starts off by being cut off, pushed away, and almost divorced by the very God who will send him, before he can speak his words of reconciliation. In a moment we will even see him sent to gentile territory to live with a pagan widow and depend on her. This makes about as much sense as a plan to save the world being based on God being murdered before he can save anyone...

... but this is the 'logic' of the text. God's thoughts are not our thoughts. Some of them do make sense from our limited perspective as we live with them and allow their wisdom to transform our thinking. Others don't seem to. However, God has no need to win our philosophical approval before taking action, and the path of vocation is first and foremost a path of obedience not mastery. This is exactly why understanding this section as panto helps. Allow it to flow! Enjoy it! Let the absurdity delight you, the profundity move you, the accusation convict you as you chuckle away at your own foolishness and come out changed.

Notice, too, that vocation that is really Godly vocation usually involves the embracing of the outcast, and often starts with the calling of the least obvious person. I talk to lots of people who think it is absurd that God is calling them (and I know how they feel).

Scene 2 (vv8-16)

Elijah moves to Zarephath in Sidon only for the miraculous to recur, this time involving a widow rather than a raven, and taking place in enemy territory. (Does the name Sidon ring a bell? Can you hear the musicians ('dun, dun, daaaah') as the actors pause in unlikely poses? Sidon has a princess by the name of Jezebel, daughter of King Ethbaal (which means 'with Baal'), and she is the one who is married to King Ahab.)

Here it is that Elijah meets a widow who has all but run out of oil and grain and is preparing the last meal she and her son will eat, and asks for water and food. He asks, and she laughs in his face and tells him to get lost...

... except that she doesn't. Listen to the actors' voices! Imagine the expressions as the actual drama plays out in front of us:

'Give me your last meal, please, kind lady.'

'We have no food, only enough for our last meal before we die.'

'That's fine, give it to me and the God of your enemies who your princess is busy debunking will look after you.'

'Oh! OK then!'

This is one of many times in this pantomime where the expected does not happen, but God turns up and meets the needs of those who trust in him. We are not wrong to laugh, and we would be foolish not to wonder.

Elijah, the widow, and her son are miraculously fed whilst the drought lasts. The diet may not be varied, but by the faith of the prophet, the trust of the widow and her son, and the miraculous provision of God, they eat well.

Scene 3 (vv17-24)

And so... well, not to beat about the bush... the widow's son dies.

Uggh: this is not what was expected, and it is not what is supposed to happen in panto (but then this isn't really panto, it's just a bit like it). Bad things happen to good people in real life and we will not always understand why. Vocation is not really pantomime, it is real world stuff, and Godly vocation does not duck real issues. It gets stuck in, and Elijah does too.

He cries out to God. He gets proper stroppy, and God hears and answers his prayer and the boy is raised from the dead. And almost as unexpectedly, the first scene draws to a close with a Sidonian widow affirming that the word of God is in the mouth of Elijah.

3. VOCATION DEFINED: MAKING THE CONNECTION

As the panto pauses for a change of scene, let's wander outside the auditorium for a drink (if you want to stay in character) and talk about what we are beginning to see. The reason we are revisiting this text is to help us think about vocation. The link is clear in my mind, but let me make it explicit so as not to leave you stranded as I appear to dart off in random directions in our evolving conversation.

In the Old Testament there were three things that you were anointed to do. You would get anointed if you were called to be a priest (Exodus 28.41, for example), a prophet (1 Kings 19.16, for example), or a king (1 Samuel 9.16, for example). God set you aside, marked you by anointing, and gave you a role and a task. Kings, in particular, were given both power and responsibility, but all three matter (which is why the 'messiah' or 'anointed one' brings all three offices together in the person of Jesus, the Christ, the Messiah, of course). As we read both of Ahab and of the prophets, we read about God calling, or in more formal terminology, about vocation.

We do get worked up about things like 'calling'; for example feeling we can only discuss it with uber-complicated terminology, or thoughtlessly expecting that God should adhere to our timetable or agenda. This, I suspect, is partly why we are given gifts like this chunk of the Bible to enjoy, inhabit, and learn from. We'll look more fully at some of the lessons we can learn later in the book, but before we do, let's think a bit about what we mean when we talk about vocation.

Vocation: some myths:

As I say, we do get worked up and worried about vocation. We hear this specific word used only in limited contexts and assume it has nothing to do with what we are called to be or to do in our context... which is mostly fine, except in this case it means we miss out.

Vocation is not just about ordination

We often assume that vocation, at least Godly vocation, is only about getting ordained or becoming a nun or a monk. It really isn't... at least it isn't only about that. If you look at 'vocation' on the Church of England website you will find these words:

Vocation means what you are called by God to be and do.

For some, this is a specific calling to ministry. For others, it could mean serving God through faithful discipleship in everyday life.

Everyone has a vocation. Find yours.

Some are called to be ordained. This is a vocation. Andy, who is my chaplain at the time of writing, is one such. He is not directly leading a church at the moment but spends most of his time at a desk or on the phone. He is an essential part of the 'Bishop of Chester' (in the bigger sense than just the person) and very much in ministry. He could do much of the role without being ordained, but he is not somehow less ordained because of that. His vocation to ordination has had various expressions thus far, and will, I am sure, have more yet. Being a chaplain is part of the vocation he is inhabiting, but don't imagine he knew he would do this role when he first felt called to be ordained. God has called, though, and he has obeyed, and I am extremely grateful to them both. Vocation evolves and has seasons.

Some are called to church roles that are not ordained, like youth workers or administrators. Rachel, my amazing PA, is another of the people who you will meet in this book. She's not ordained, but I am in no doubt that God has called her to her professional role which uses her gifts and abilities and gives her a platform to serve the LORD and so many people in ways that few others could match. She enables parts of my work in ways I couldn't. Partly this is technical: she is good at stuff. Partly it is character: she brings the best out of people as she interacts with them in this role. Partly it is personality: she either really loves what she does or is a great actor. Partly it is the way that she seems able to do the role for Jesus not just for herself, the church, or for me. I rely on her at least as much as I do on Andy and have no doubt at all that this is a role she is called to, but the vocational 'box' is far less easy to describe for her.

Some are called to roles both in and out of the church. I am married to Lindsay who is a senior Social Worker in her 'working life' and a Reader (like a lay preacher) in the Church of England. Some people seem to believe that her vocation is to be a Reader who pops out to do a bit of social work in her spare time. She is a great Reader, but as you can hear when you meet her, her overall vocation is massively shaped by her call to Social Work. I don't know how she does it given all the pressures and demands: obviously she is superhuman and wonderful (not that I am biased), but mainly she is called, equipped, and empowered by God. Again, the skewing of our understanding of vocation as if it only really values church-based ministry seems problematic to me.

Others have no formal role in the church, but they are called to be parents, or to work the tills in Morrisons, or to craft metal in a smithy. In the drama we have just unpacked we see at least two vocations (Prophet and King, and later we ought *both* to be surprised at Elijah anointing a foreign king *and* notice that this emphasises exactly the point that Kingship is vocation). There are others who are clearly called though. What about Obadiah's vocation to service, or the widow of Zarephath's vocation as a mother, for example?

Vocation is not just for posh people or high-profile careers

I choose these latter examples because the other error we often make is to assume that vocation is a posh name for an important job. It is easy to think people can have a vocation to teach. Or to be a lawyer. Or be a doctor. It is far less straightforward (or at least far less common) to explore vocation to be a lollypop lady (as I was discussing with the most remarkable Christian woman earlier in the year who has invited me to join her at her crossing for a morning: I am unreasonably excited about this), or to be a great delivery driver, or to be a foster-mum for the honour of Christ and witness to his grace.

Really, though, those careers that talk vocation are just the ones which have been around for ages, where the work was steady enough to do it for a lifetime, and where people knew a bit of Latin so they understood the terminology. We need to do better here: vocation is simply about God calling you to something or somethings. Because God is very good, very kind, and knows you very well, there is nothing better than finding God's call, your vocation, and all Christians need this.

Vocation is not the same as 'job' or even 'career'

Because we often make the first two mistakes, we, at least I, often make the mistake of effectively equating 'job' and 'vocation'. Have a look through the pages later in the book where you meet different people and hear about their understanding of vocation; you will repeatedly see how unhelpful it is to muddle these two up. The trouble is, though, that the idea is like some kind of siren to the soul, alluring, misleading, and ultimately dangerous. We can easily look at others and think that they are sorted because 'God told them what to do with their life.' At a passing glance, a teacher looks like they are simply a teacher, a vicar simply like a vicar, a doctor like a doctor and so on... vocation is more than this though.

This is one of the many reasons, incidentally, why we who hog the term 'vocation' (like vicars) need to share it more and learn from others. Think about it for a moment. I was ordained in my twenties, but I had already worked before that (as a youth worker, on the farm, and at various other bitty things). Did my vocation start when the bishop laid his hands on my head? I don't think so. Since being ordained I have been a curate (an assistant vicar, learning the ropes and working in a local church), led a couple of churches, established some new church communities, been a chaplain for the army, run a theological college alongside a role in the University, chaired too many trustee bodies to count, been a suffragan (like an assistant) bishop, written a few things, and now lead a diocese alongside bits of national work. Which of these are my vocation? Running an SME? Being a preacher/teacher/spiritual director? Serving in the clear structures of the military? Being an academic, or an author?

Doing administration? I have had many jobs, even more roles, and all whilst being ordained.

The same would be true of my dad. He worked as a doctor for the whole of his working life, but this involved clinical work, research, teaching, writing, and oversight of many others as they learned and worked in clinical and research fields.

There is even more than this, here, though. These examples could give the impression that, whilst 'vocation' is not the same as 'job', it is a career. I have had many 'jobs' since being ordained, but in some senses have had one career (although we don't usually talk about a 'career' in the church). It is true that a career will often express more of a person's vocation than any one job; it is usually more varied and longer. However, this is still a dangerous equation. Someone's 'career' does not usually include a vocation to marriage or parenthood, for example, but those are vital parts of the vocation of those called to them. I think of a friend who clearly has a vocation to youth work, but whose career is as a highly skilled craftsman. Their 'volunteer' activity with young people is as much part of their overall vocation as the wonders they create in the workshop.

It is, of course true, that some have a guiding overall 'vocation to' something (I have no doubt I have had a vocation to be ordained, for example) whilst others won't in quite the same way, but it would be foolish to think that this closes the vocational question.

Why do I say 'foolish' (as my finger hovers over the delete key and I decide to leave that word in the text)? Partly because it would be wrong. Partly because it is such an easy mistake to make and we later regret it, I think. Mainly because if we do this we miss out on so much. Those who find themselves in a traditional 'vocation' miss out on the vocational tools that could have helped them decide which opportunities to pursue within it and which to leave out. Those whose path lies outside one of the careers others might describe as vocational can find themselves devalued (which is bad enough), but also cut off from the learning about vocation which ought to be part of our inheritance as Christians.

Vocation: some truths

Here are some basic truths about vocation:

'Vocation' simply means...

... what you are called to. As Christians, we believe it is God who does the calling, of course. There are so many reasons why it matters to know that we are called to something by God. Here are a few:

- When God calls, he also equips. I can't remember when or where I first heard that, but it is true. Most people who are doing tough things struggle at times to do them (to state the obvious); one of the many gifts of

God is to strengthen, enrich, enable, and give grace beyond ourselves.

- When we know we are called it gives us a reason to carry on. I sometimes wonder if what I am doing is really worth it but knowing that God has called does encourage and affirm what I am doing. If my vocation is firstly about service to him then what I do is offered as an act of worship and service.
- Similarly, knowing I am called gives me confidence that it will work out even when I don't know quite how.

God is in the calling and partnership business...

... in a pretty obvious way. This is clear when we look at history and at the Bible. It is pretty amazing though when you think about it! He really doesn't have to be. He is big enough to do this by himself, but he chooses partnership (I think it is something to do with his nature being love, but that's another book).

You are created in his image.

So, vocation is actually about discovering who you are designed to be. Partnering with God. In God's work.

More than that, though, God chooses all manner of partnerships in order to carry out his work around our world, and urgently seeks people to partner with him in doing the work, becoming good at it, and training others to do the same.

Vocation usually refers to long-term calling...

... but not always life-long. We don't really bother about calling short-term callings 'vocation' (although technically I guess they are things that we are called to as well). We use the term for bigger stuff, where we devote ourselves in response to a deep call of God on our life. This is genuine partnership where we are allowed to contribute to God's work and not only play in the light of his kindness.

Inhabiting vocation takes discipline, practice, training, imagination, and skill. It might be caught quickly but it will usually develop slowly. It is not a job so much as a lifestyle, not a task so much as an approach to being. It brings meaning and purpose and makes a difference.

And, very often, it seems to me that those who are most vocationally shaped don't feel that they are very good at what they do. I am not sure I can explain this, except that I notice three things:

1) When you inhabit a vocation, you have a hunger for perfection in that area and therefore it seems blindly obvious to you when you fall short.
2) In particular you work hard on the stuff that irritates you most about yourself, at one and the same time getting much better at it and much more irritated at the little things you get wrong.
3) This keeps Godly people humble, which seems to keep many of my heroes real, approachable, and nice to be with.

All of this means that others are often better at spotting your vocation than you are, of course, but it also means that we need to dedicate ourselves over the long term to follow vocational identity. How desperately do we need to rediscover this in our generation which so often seems concerned only with results, wealth, and image?

All vocations are valuable...

... because of the One who calls us into them. We are pretty rubbish at recognising this, but it is deeply true. It leads me to ask how I value others and also how I learn to value my own vocation. It is so easy to place ourselves in a kind of 'pecking order' and it is rarely helpful.

In my current role people often seem to ask me if I am happy. I have no idea why, although we do have had some tough stuff to deal with. If there is time to be frank with them, I tend to explain that I am less and less sure that 'happiness' is the point of life, but that I am deeply content. Contentment comes from knowing that you are in the right place at the right time and with the right people. That you are doing something worthwhile and making a bit of a difference. That, whilst you might feel like a little bit of a wazzock sometimes, you really are learning, growing, and helping people. That you are loved, and that you have the privilege of loving people in a way that blesses them. And that you have discovered your vocation... you are at home. This is a vital secret to be grasped (and I am just at the start of doing so, lest I give you the wrong impression).

Vocation is about gifts not just abilities…

… although abilities matter too. This is the thing I think I talk about most with people who are searching for their own vocation. I say this for two reasons; one about how we inhabit vocation and the other about how we discern it.

In terms of inhabiting vocation, we are so often tempted to do God's job for him. We offer our service as if we are doing him a favour and clearing up some stuff for an elderly relative. Quite a lot gets done like this in the church, to be honest, but I am not sure God heaves a sigh of relief when we roll into view with our superb skill at [insert your greatest ability here]. However good you are at telling jokes to 5-year-olds, creating a spreadsheet, or catering for 400+ people (and I admire all of those skills) I am pretty sure that God would beat you in a bake-off style showdown.

Gifts, though, are a bit different. (I am not really using the terms technically here, merely trying to describe what I see.) A gift, in my language, is an ability, but it is somehow inhabited by the Holy Spirit of the living God; it is restored by love, shaped by God's restless energy, outward focussed, and life-giving both to giver and recipient. Some abilities just never seem to function that way. There are some things that I reluctantly accept I am quite good at, but I could never really be satisfied spending my life doing them. I am reasonably good at organising people, I guess, but there would be a high risk of fisticuffs by day 2 if I tried to be a PA. There are other things that I hear I do OK at (even though by my reckoning I am stunningly mediocre) which bring life to others and to me. I love preaching, for example, and rarely tire of that task. I notice one of the key differences is that, pretty much every time I stand up to preach, I find myself in a quiet moment with Jesus re-mentioning that unless he takes over we are sunk, whereas when I organise people I just get a bit grumpy that they can't sort themselves out. I am not proud of it and try to be nicer, but it does happen all too often (at least internally).

Both gifts and abilities matter, and both need to be devoted to God's service. You will often be called upon to do stuff because you are the right person at the right place in the right moment. Vocation, though, is shaped far more by your gifts, I think, than your abilities. Gifts are shared. Abilities are owned. Gifts often energise, ability can weary. Gifts inspire, ability can conspire or show off. Gifts release, abilities control. Gifts usually take trusting faith to exercise; abilities showcase our own talent. Of course, I am being overly black and white in trying to capture something here, but your vocation will not always be shaped only by the stuff you feel good at; God loves you more than this. Vocation is held in partnership (usually both with God and with others) and we need to work on the freedom to inhabit our gifts and worry less when we find ourselves out of our depth in our following of Christ.

It is also worth noticing that this gift/ability distinction can help us discern where vocation lies. Many people are just too good at too much stuff and could do pretty much anything given the right opportunities. However, not everything gives them life. It seems to me that reflecting on gifts is a good, although far from infallible, reflection of the Spirit witnessing to what God is already doing in us. We were created to cooperate with God, and something inside us sings when we are doing so. There is loads of stuff we just need to get done, which is not sinful or wrong but is just stuff. It can be joyful just as it can be mundane, but it will never form the heartbeat of your life. Living out your gifting and calling though; that brings life even when it is tough as tough can be. Repeated conversation with different types of people over the years makes me think that folk seem to recognise this once it is described, even when the description is as hard to capture as I find it to be.

Vocation evolves

Finally, I want to note that vocation evolves. Talking of it as we do might imply that it is a static thing, but it really isn't. It is living, dynamic, and it develops. I use the word 'evolve' because its fundamental character remains constant, but its expression and identity will look different as years go by. Be careful of allowing your vocation to become too closely identified with a particular role, title, place, or group. They can (and will) all change, but God has not finished with you yet. This can be one of the hardest things for even the most experienced Christians to grasp in practice, it seems, but it is vital to recognise. Circumstances change, but vocation remains and matures and develops.

Vocation: a caveat

There is one slight danger I want to point out before we move on. There is a danger that 'vocation' might come to feel a bit more slippery as you think about it through this book before it becomes clearer. It would be simple if we could either say something very specific, like 'my vocation is to write the music for the new James Bond film', but we have noted that this is too tight a concept to be helpful. That may be part of your vocation, although I doubt it is part of mine, but such specificity will rarely capture the sweep of the call of God on your life.

Equally, it is possible to be so broad that the conversation is not helpful. All Christians, for example, have a vocation to forgive. For some, in some situations, this general facet of vocation might become vitally important and be a real focus. However, 'forgiveness' may not be an altogether useful overall definition of vocation for many of us (although there are those called into conflict resolution for whom it may well be).

It is likely, I think, that we need to learn to hold vocation both more loosely than we would like to and more tightly than we are accustomed to, for such is the nature of a dynamic relationship with the living God. Arguably this is part of what we see as difference between Ahab and the prophets. The prophets are responsive, adaptable, and willing. As we shall see, Ahab has a fixed (and wrong) idea about Kingship and believes himself to be at liberty to pursue it as he wishes. Vocation should never be reified: it must always be God himself that we pursue, never the thing that he holds out to us: the giver matters infinitely more than the gift in any relationship of love.

Vocation: some Anglican observations about ordination, lay ministry, and other stuff

We need to be clear, then, that vocation is not just about ordination. It includes and embraces the whole gamut of life and this is vital.

Neither is it only about the 'stuff' that happens in the church (ordained or lay church-based ministry and the religious life). Indeed, ministry itself is not only about the things that happen in church: I think we have made this point and we need to keep making it.

In the Church of England this is made more complicated, though, by fact that we seem to be in a bit of a practical muddle about vocations to ordination, lay ministry, and religious life. I feel a bit cautious saying this given that I have just become chair of the Ministry Council of the Church of England, but I am not really trying to do anything more than name what I see.

Let's start with religious life, being a monk or nun: I have been a bishop in the Church of England for six years now and supported well over a hundred people going forward to ordained ministry and about the same number into some kind of recognised Lay Ministry. I can't find any statistics (which is probably telling in itself), but I can only think of one person who has even explored the religious life under my care. Our religious communities are shrinking, aging, and closing, and yet we know in our heart of hearts that we value them.

It is possible that God is closing down our religious communities, but I deeply hope not. I am not sure we have any real shared sense of what it means to have a religious vocation today, and worry that we are not co-operating with the Spirit in these matters.

And then let's think about ordained ministry. We have three orders of ordained ministry, deacon, priest (or presbyter), and bishop. We can't even agree what to call the middle of the three. We allow people to feel called to be a priest, look at them with great suspicion if they express a calling to be a bishop, and have little imagination when it comes to long-term distinctive diaconate (which is what we call it when people are called to serve as deacons for the long-term). In 2020 there were 20,000 ordained ministers in the Church of England according to our statistics. 150 of these were Distinctive Deacons, less than 1%.

In a world which desperately needs radical servant ministry, I worry that we only see diaconal ministry as a foundation for priestly ministry (and possibly not even that).

We have over twenty training institutions for ordained ministry, and they vary hugely on their understanding of what a priest (or presbyter) is and does. You could spend the morning in North London and be fairly sure that people were being trained to minister in the free Evangelical church, and drive an hour to spend the afternoon in Oxford and worry that those being trained might be too sacramental to fit into the Roman Catholic Church.

I don't fret about this, personally speaking. We hold together around the ordinal (the service where people are ordained), which tells us that Priests are ordained to lead, to set an example based on Christ, and to be faithful servants and shepherds. They are to tell the story of God's love, to baptise, to 'unfold' the scriptures, to preach, to preside at Holy Communion and to lead worship. They are to pray, to support, and to be guided by the Holy Spirit, among many other things (the full text is available from the Church of England website). They are to foster unity, grace and love.

I am of the view that we have a sufficient theology and definition of priesthood, but we do need to be clearer about what our understanding actually means. (This is not a view that all would share, incidentally, I have not heard many others espouse it.) To my mind, when you combine the ordinal with the great traditions of the church you end up with pretty much what we have in terms of ordained ministry, from evangelical to catholic, charismatic to liberal, and everything in between. We should not worry about this as most practical theology is the result of different theological insights bumping into each other. I am not sure that we can write a distinctive or substantive theology of church planting, for example, but hold ecclesiology, missiology, and sociology together for any length of time and you rapidly realise that some kind of church planting practice is needed in in order to live out the consequences of the first two in the reality of the third.

Ordination is not about robes, tasks, titles, or jobs. It is an ordered, stable, and covenanted, ministerial relationship with God's church, mediated through the Bishop, which is long-term, sustainable, resourced, pastoral, and missional and at the same time structures our worship, maintains orthodoxy and unity, supports the ordained, releases the people of God to service, and enables appropriate accountability. That's what the ordinal says, I think.

So, speaking purely personally, I don't have too much of a problem with our theology of ordination. I do think that our practice of discerning and fostering diaconal vocation is deeply problematic, but that is not my biggest concern theologically or ecclesiologically when it comes to ministerial vocation. I don't want to be contentious, but I do think we are in a muddle about some lay ministry and we don't know how to wrestle with it because we don't like offending people... and this matters because lay ministry really matters.

I am surrounded on a daily basis by three people I have already mentioned, Andy, Lindsay, and Rachel, one ordained, one licensed lay, and one lay. Each of the three has a clear vocation, two are lay, two are ministerial (in a public worship sense), but all spend most of their life at the moment at computers doing administration. Lindsay occupies that fascinating lay ministerial space of public ministry in the church alongside a demanding 'secular' career (I am not sure it really is secular, but suspect you know what I mean) which enables all manner of bridges to be built, connections to be made, and mission to happen. Rachel has a deeply significant ministry caring for many folk around the diocese, but is not currently licensed let alone ordained. Andy is ordained but is not currently running a church. The difference between them is in the relationship they have with the church, not the value of their ministry.

I rejoice in the variety of ministry that the Church of England is now trying to embrace, resource, and explore. Nationally we see this in projects like 'Kingdom Calling'. Locally we see it in all sorts of ways. Rachel and Lindsay are good examples of this, perhaps, although there are good and continuing questions about how we as church support the Social Work part of a vocation like Lindsay's. However, it does bamboozle me a bit when people want to be life-long overall ministerial church leaders within the Church of England but do so as a lay person. I confess that I do not know what this means, and no-one seems able to explain it to me, except that they 'do not feel called to be ordained'. It seems to me that this raises troubling questions about both ordination and lay ministry: about ordination because we seem to have created a grouping which is about something other than ministerial service, and about lay ministry because there appears to be an unexamined (or at least not persuasive) assertion that a non-ordained model of leadership brings missing gifts without the need for covenanted relationship with the church through the Bishop, ordered relationship with fellow ministers, theological education, or long-term commitment.

I suspect that we need to be willing to examine the questions this raises, if we really want to affirm and enable lay vocation, but also if we want to continue to support ordained vocation and order. We are probably not flexible enough, and the danger with settled systems is that they usually find new questions uncomfortable even when they are needed.

Another matter that worries me, now that I have started, is that we seem obsessed with titles. This amuses me in most instances, but does worry me when it comes to breaking new ground. I love pioneers and the pioneering that they do. We need more. It does surprise me, though, the pressure that some people place on me to license them as pioneers before they are pioneering. I always ask what they are pioneering, and some look at me askance, preferring to tell me about the training that they have done or how the church should be different to make space for them. The training is great, and the church must always keep developing, but 'pioneer' in missional terms is a verb long before it is a noun, so I ask again what they are pioneering. People seem both surprised and offended when I indicate that they can be licensed as a pioneer if they want to be, but not until they are pioneering something.

I emphasise this not to try to make a clever point, but rather because we need to stay focussed on the mission with which we have been entrusted. Mission is tough. Church can be tough, but mission is harder. People 'out there' don't care much about titles (no-one knows that most people in clerical collars are not actually 'Vicar' for example), they care if people make a difference. I care about this and I care about how we support the whole people of God as they serve the whole mission of God.

There are real questions of vocation for us as a church, but they are not about stereotypes, titles, or the latest 'thing'. We urgently need to work on how we enable the people of God to explore, inhabit, and share all that God is calling them to.

We urgently need to cherish the breadth, depth, and wonder of holy orders, and release the extraordinary gift of lay vocation and lay ministry (those are two different things). We don't need to get it 100% right and it will never be neat, but neither is it really about us... and the one whom it is all about has so much more up his sleeves than we can begin to imagine or hope for.

Anyway, the bell has rung, let's get back in for the next act... it's a good 'un.

4. PANTO ACT 2:
ELIJAH AND AHAB (1 KINGS 18.1-19.2)

As the lights fade up, we, as modern readers, relax into familiarity. This is the 'to be or not to be' bit of the play that everyone knows, the 'hallelujah chorus' that we have sung along to since Sunday School. There are lots of 'valid' ways to read this story, however, when we pause and enjoy it, we might glimpse this midrash-morality-panto-take on the story we thought we knew. It is funnier, more violent, more perplexing, and more amazing than we realised as kids (if we were blessed enough to hear it then): few kids' club leaders mentioned the hundreds of religious executions in verse 40 or the fact that Elijah was actually outnumbered 850 to one when the additional 400 'prophets' of Asherah mentioned in verse 19 are taken into account.

(You might like to know that Baal was the god of rain, wind, and fertility. Asherah was the goddess of motherhood and fertility. She was thought be either Baal's mother, lover, or both. Judging by the statues and carvings of them which still survive, if they appeared on stage the censors would increase the age-rating of this show considerably. This may influence the way you view this act of the panto, but I point it out because vocation does not duck out of confronting complex or troubling issues.)

Scene 1 (vv1-16)

The act begins, though, with God telling Elijah to meet Ahab for the second time (at least in the text): there was to be no rain until I said so... but now, listen up and take notice! Rain is coming. True to form, Elijah obeys, and off he trots... but first a cameo appearance for Obadiah.

We don't know much about this Obadiah. It was a common(ish) name at the time, meaning 'servant' or 'worker', and appearing 19 times in the Old Testament and a couple more in the apocryphal books of Esdras. Some teachers assert that this is the Obadiah who wrote the eponymous biblical book, which would mean that he, too, is a prophet in that he had visions and earned his player's cap on the field with the rest of the 'minor prophets' at the close of play of the Hebrew Scriptures.

We don't know that for certain, but he was clearly a servant of the King, clearly faithful to God, clearly bold and obedient.

Jezebel bobs onto stage at this point ('boo, hiss, she's behind you...') killing the prophets of the LORD, but Obadiah hides a hundred of them to save their lives. There are a lot of prophets in the wings of this drama, but it is notable that the big numbers are of little consequence; this passage is about the key players and the lessons that they teach to the faithful. The Bible often portrays God as preferring a genuine encounter with named individuals rather than with 'everybody': he knows, loves, and calls real people like you.

Obadiah is bold, faithful, and deeply human. He meets Elijah whilst he is out on the king's command looking for fresh grass. He assumes Elijah is about to betray him, either by handing him over to Ahab to be killed or by hiding once Obadiah has told Ahab where Elijah is. It is interesting to eavesdrop on this conversation between prophets who are meant to be on the same side. Shared vocation does not always mean that it is easy to trust each other, although this is a good model of how we should overcome suspicion and fear in this regard. Talk about it, acknowledge it, choose a different course.

Scene 2 (vv17-19)

As promised, though, Elijah and Ahab meet, and it's a bit tense. We probably need a bit of set-piece comedy to break the tension, and that is coming, but first we get a slam-dunk of profundity: verse 18 is set up by Ahab's friendly greeting. When Ahab saw Elijah, Ahab said to him, 'Is it you, you troubler of Israel?'"

Elijah replies: "I have not troubled Israel; but you have, and your father's house, because you have forsaken the commandments of the LORD and followed the Baals." Here is the core of the issue. The king has failed to be a king and he stands in a line with those who have forgotten what kingship is. They have ousted God, forsaken the people, and put themselves central to the monarchy, the nation, and the destiny of God's people. This is deeply serious stuff. It is the root of the problem, and the issue that this whole section of the Bible revolves around.

Panto, though, cannot stay serious for long... at least at surface level. The spotlight has shone on the problem, but it will move on for a while and let us laugh at Ahab, at Jezebel (if we are bloodthirsty), at Elijah even, but always draw us back to the question of faithfulness. And so we quickly move to the set-piece that comprises most of Chapter 18. Too often this is preached seriously, and in one way it should be, but only in the way that comedy is sometimes deadly serious. This is hilarious, slapstick, showdown. Even toddlers can get the point here. This is David and Goliath, parting of the Red Sea, CAPITAL LETTERS kind of teaching where the point is obvious and the story is meant to be enjoyed. It should be learned, chanted, laughed over, and retold. Even an idiot can get the point, especially when God ends the drought immediately afterwards... but Ahab, great King Ahab, slinks off back to Jezebel. Jezebels are very attractive, but they aren't very good for vocation.

However, we jump ahead; let's enjoy the show.

Scene 3 (vv20-40)

So... here we are on the mountain top. The familiar theme song strikes up, beat thumping, audience starts clapping in time. This is feel-good, rabble-rousing, heart-pumping stuff. Here is Elijah in the shiny suit only used for this scene, and he loves that every eye is on him. No-one cares that it is larger than life: that is the point. There is a fundamental truth to be grasped here, and it cannot be contained in the mind, in our liturgy, or even just in our creeds: this is part of the foundation of life itself... so buckle up.

Elijah mocks: 'how long will you limp around?' (v21)

Elijah exaggerates his own insignificance, whipping the crowd to a frenzy: 'I, even I...' (can you see him owning the stage as he pauses dramatically and points derisively to himself at this point? Someone calls out... Give me an 'E...', 'E – L – I – J – A – H') '... I, even I, am the only prophet of the LORD' (v22), even though we have been told in verse 4 that good old Obadiah has saved another 100 of them and we will be introduced to others in each of the succeeding chapters.

Elijah plays to the crowd as he sets up a very public spectacle with the two sacrifices and lets the false prophets go first.

Elijah taunts. Boy, does he taunt. Even in English the mockery comes over: 'maybe he is asleep or travelling... shout a little louder' (v27) as they 'limp' around the altar they have made clearly portrayed as ridiculous. Apparently, the Hebrew is even ruder, or at least open to far ruder interpretation: 'shout a bit louder: he's in the khazi', 'speak up, your so-called God has had to whip off for a slash (that's how much he cares about you)', or even 'he's gone for a dump, so be patient he might be a while...'. All of these seem to be the crude metaphorical understandings that the original hearers would have understood. Some scholars even suggest that the text implies that Elijah is suggesting that Baal is distracted by amusing himself rather than listening to all the wailing prophets, which may offend modern readers (although could fit quite well with bawdy panto and the even bawdier statues that survive of both Baal and Asherah), but does pick up exactly the contrast between the faithful, kind, and loving attention of the LORD and the abusive disinterest of the Baals. And, what's more, even though I don't feel able to write it, you can kind of hear the actor chanting 'Baal is a ******' with an appropriate clash of cymbals to cover the rude word each time it is said.

Elijah goes on building the tension. He doesn't even start repairing the LORD's altar until after all the other activity is done and dusted. He works carefully, piles it high, and then drenches it repeatedly in water. Might there even be a replay of the urination taunt here: 'your so-called god was off having a wee, let me show you what the true God thinks of that'?

And God turns up: fire, worship, confession (and mass execution). God has won. The point is made. In Hollywood, the credits would roll, the curtain would close, and Elijah would exit stage left pursued by a bearer of fan letters. There wouldn't be the killings either of course: my best guess is that, depending on whether a sequel was planned, the false prophets would either convert en masse and set up a popular worship band or they would glare meaningfully at the beloved Elijah leaving us in no doubt that they would be back.

The vocation of the prophet is altogether more real than this though, and this act is not yet finished.

Scene 4 (18.41-19.2)

Re-enter Elijah onto stage: no longer in sequins but blood-spattered and in his executioner's robes, no longer in the public eye but alone with the king. To be honest this scene is a little dark and Ahab would be foolish not to be scared. He does, at least, do as he is told and go off to eat and drink (v42). It's the opening chat that intrigues, though. Elijah tells Ahab that there is the sound of rushing rain (v41), even though later the poor old servant will have to look seven times before he even sees a cloud as big as a human hand in the sky. Clearly this is a prophetic statement but, as with Micaiah in Chapter 22, it speaks of a different reality in a manner that seems at odds with current truth. From the cheap seats we do not pick up the dialogue between Elijah and God. We cannot always hear the conversation that lies behind another's vocation to prophecy, which means that vocation is often a work of trust, but it is not an untested work of trust.

Ahab cannot, of course, hear the rain either, but by the end of the day his chariot will hardly be able to move because of the mud, and the journey he then takes is telling. I am intrigued by Elijah's super-athleticism here as he girds his loins and outruns Ahab, but the more intriguing thing is why Ahab heads back to Jezebel. The whole point of this Act is that the LORD is good and the

Baals are bad. Jezebel has been discredited but back Ahab goes and with him his kingship.

Make no mistake here: Ahab is given every opportunity to reform his vocation. We will see more later, but he makes the choice to return. Is he foolish? Is he wicked? We don't really know, but what we do know is that he is responsible. Jezebel has been demonised down the ages: she is a wicked foreign woman and easy to write off in a world full of everyday misogyny and blind racism, but she is not wicked because she is foreign and neither is she evil because she is a woman. In this dramatic retelling of history she is a deliberate stereotype: she is set up as the personification of anti-God. There is little doubt that she did follow other Gods, I am not suggesting this is false narrative, but the dramatic effect here is to make Ahab's (and in a moment Elijah's) choice clear. We cannot place the blame for our failure of vocation on a convenient other. Ahab is to blame for his own mistakes, and Jezebel for hers... and they egg each other on.

For this act, like the first, ends with the words of a Sidonian woman (19.2). This word, though, is not affirming but threatening, not grateful but furious, not from a convert but from an enemy of the living God, and once again this one has an impact.

Just as we need to be clear who is at fault in these passages, so we need to note the responsibility on all of the actors to be careful about those to whom they choose to listen or give attention. In the brief interludes in these chapters where Ahab appears to respond without listening to Jezebel there is hope, but this is not the run of play. Here, to exaggerated effect that sits four-square on the pantomime stage we are describing, Ahab allows his life to be shaped by Jezebel, the personification of evil who is the wicked step-sister (wife in this case, actually, but all the best pantos have nasty step-sisters). In a moment Elijah will do likewise.

5. PANTO ACT 3
A ROAD TRIP AND A MOUNTAIN
(1 KINGS 19)

Jezebel's words echo at the start of Act 3. Having heard what Elijah did to her pet prophets, she responds: 'So may the gods do to me, and more also, if I do not make your life like the life of one of them by this time tomorrow.' (v1)

Scene 1 (19.3-8)

We in the audience are pumped up. We have seen the triumph of Act 2 and are buzzing with Elijah's heroism. 'Bring it on', we want to shout. 'Come and have a go if you think you're hard enough...' We have seen what happens to those 'gods' when they go head-to-head with the God of Elijah and round two is fine by us. We are waiting for Elijah to stand and make himself clear.

'What gods would they be then, Jezza? Your barmy-baals? The ones I have just given a good kicking around the mountain top? Bring it on...'

This is, I think, the logic of the text.

Except he doesn't say that, do that, or even appear to think that.

He listens to Jezebel, believes her, is terrified and he flees for his life to such an extent that he even needs to be virtually force-fed food by God to strengthen him for the journey. He hears, and he runs to the middle of nowhere, abandons his servant, and goes a day further into the wilderness, sits under a lonely tree and hopes to die...

'It is enough; now, O LORD, take away my life, for I am no better than my ancestors.' (v4)

He will return to this theme after a long walk. Clearly it is a settled mindset and no mere passing thought. He withdraws, he loses his focus, he becomes fixated on Jezebel's words, he complains, and he sleeps; I am no expert and it is always dangerous to read modern concepts too strictly back into the biblical text, but this sounds remarkably like depression to me. Elijah is still human.

God meets and feeds him (more precisely 'the Angel of the LORD' does so, but it is commonly held that this is code for God himself. Even if it isn't, clearly this is a direct emissary from God who is caring for Elijah). Indeed, he has to rouse him and persuade him to eat more than he is naturally inclined to do. Moreover, God knows the journey that Elijah must take before Elijah does, and (unlike Ahab) Elijah obeys and sets off.

Humanly speaking, he takes some time out; spiritually speaking he heads off to meet with God. He walks alone and the text is silent for forty days (which some suggest is just code for 'a long time' but would have felt like ages whichever way around). As we reflect seriously on a text which presents comedically (albeit for serious consumption) we are wise to remember that there is much to the lives of all the characters that is hidden. I mention this for three reasons: one to remind us that each vocation is unique and will not be fully grasped by others, another is to note that God does not give up on us when we feel we have failed in our vocation, and thirdly to point out that we have the rest of the Bible alongside this chunk. Inhabiting this comedy, as and when we inhabit it as comedy, is done with the seriousness both of this text and the wider canon in mind and heart.

Scene 2 (vv9-18)

So, Elijah arrives at the cave on the mountain. We are not told how he knows where to go, except that he has headed to the 'mount of God' (v8). This is an archetypal place informed by the instinct of the faithful to seek the presence of God and instinctively understood by the audience (at least the original audience). They know where he is and they know what he is to expect. Jokes are always ruined by explaining them, of course, but in this place you can bet your bottom Shekel that:

1) God will 'turn up' as he did repeatedly to Moses (see Exodus 3.1 for example)
2) That when he turns up one of three things is likely to happen (theologians call these signs of 'theophany', but I am already ruining the joke by explaining it; the last thing I need to do is bring a theologian on stage at this point):
    a) There will be wind (think of creation (Genesis 1.2) or the parting of the Red Sea (Exodus 14)),
    b) The ground would shake (which we see, for example in Isaiah 2.19-21 or in Psalm 29.8, both of which appear later in the Bible but may well precede these events in historical terms), or
    c) There will be fire (think of the burning bush (Exodus 3), God leading through a pillar of fire (Exodus 13), or just the last chapter on Mount Moriah).

3) That Elijah will be terrified because he is human and the Hebrew Scriptures are clear that people can't look directly at God.

The text starts gently; it is the word of the LORD that comes to Elijah, although even God seems playful: His opening question 'What are you doing here, Elijah?' (v9) could be taken in a number of ways, but it clearly matters as it is repeated in verse 13 when God himself appears. Surely God already knows what Elijah is doing there? It cannot be much of a surprise to see him. Is it exasperation? Is it teasing? Whatever it is, it certainly expresses interest and gives Elijah a chance to respond.

Elijah does not hold back. There is none of the formality that we see in some of the great prayers of the Bible or the eloquent liturgy of the church. The response is basically: 'I'm fed up... brassed off... you have gone too far' as he builds on his thoughts from scene 1 with words that he will repeat verbatim in scene 3 and says 'I have been very zealous for the LORD, the God of hosts; for the Israelites have forsaken your covenant, thrown down your altars, and killed your prophets with the sword. I alone am left, and they are seeking my life, to take it away.' (v10). These feel like the words he has been brewing as he walks. God has let him stew and now invites both barrels.

It does not look good for Elijah, though: no-one talks to God like this and lives. Then it gets worse. God tells him to 'Go out and stand on the mountain before the LORD, for the LORD is about to pass by.' You can almost hear the audience shout 'No! You can't see the face of God and live', but at the same time taking a deep breath: Moses did! What are we about to see? How can this make sense?

And then there is the wind, and not just any wind. This wind splits mountains. It breaks rocks. It is before the LORD (v11). The climax of the story is about to arrive for good or ill.

But the LORD is not in the wind.

And then there is an earthquake (v11).

But the LORD is not in the earthquake... and we begin to wonder if we are being played with.

But then there is a fire (v12) and we see not just signs of God being there but three signs and EVERYONE knows that three is the number of God. So we wait.

Are we waiting for the gruesome thrill of Elijah getting smitten for running away? Or turning out to be on a par with Moses so we can wonder and adore? Or God doing something unexpected? I don't think we quite know, as we hold our breath in the auditorium and you could hear a pin drop.

But the LORD is not in the fire.

And then there is sheer silence (v12).

This does not even accord with the rules of panto. Silence doesn't work on stage. It doesn't work in conversation. It doesn't work in comforting, confrontation, or conversion... except that it does, actually, now you mention it. And the absurdity of this encounter somehow makes more sense than we have any right to expect or normal methods of communication could ever get across: God is here.

And everything changes.

The facts might still be the same. The question and the complaint are revoiced (vv13-14), but now they are held together and beyond the constraints of human fear. Elijah is recommissioned, renewed, and restored, and sets off transformed by this unexpected and absurd meeting.

And again, in direct contrast to Ahab, Elijah obeys.

Scene 3 (vv19-21)

So he goes. We don't hear about Hazael (which means 'God has seen' in Hebrew) being anointed King of Aram, even though he is to be king over an enemy of Israel: fascinating story though that might be, it is for another time. (He turns up in 2 Kings 8 where he murders his predecessor to become king and 2 Kings 12 where he receives all God's holy treasure as a bribe, but don't get me started: that is a different panto for another time.)

Neither do we hear much about Jehu, son of Nimshi (which has to be one of the best names in the Bible). Jehu is quite a common name, but he is (re)anointed on Elisha's instruction in 2 Kings 9, then proclaimed king, and later complimented on his driving style (see 2 Kings 9.20).

What we do hear is that Elijah raises up Elisha to succeed him. As I say, I have no idea how we would diagnose Elijah's mental health with a three-millennium time lapse, but some suggest that he was depressed for most of this chapter. We are not told much detail of what his plummeting lack of confidence looked like, although it would fit with a mental health concern. However, it is notable that the gift God gives in response is space, reassurance and the support of a colleague, companion, and friend.

I have often noticed in ministry, as in life, that loneliness can be cancerous. Aloneness is often good, sometimes essential, and needs to be respected, but loneliness is soul-gnawingly different. It is most unclear how and why one turns into the other or, indeed, how they are linked: I, for one, often feel most lonely when surrounded by people. But loneliness matters and should be attended to; it corrodes vocation.

6. VOCATION ABANDONED: AHAB'S APPROACH

Time for another interlude, but a rather more serious one now as we step back into the bar, grab a drink, and reflect. I do hope that you are enjoying the pantomime, and that Ahab is successfully winding you up as we reflect on vocation: God calling people into specific and long-term service. Ahab is awful but is also a gift as we learn about vocation from this section of the Bible, so let's think about what we have seen (and look forward to what we will see). Here, and in the next interval, we are going to dismantle the show from a couple of perspectives and see what we notice as we consider our own (and others') vocation. We start with Ahab and the shadow side of faithful following, with the character who abandons his own vocation in search of his own self-promotion and betterment.

Ahab is set up here as a two-dimensional, almost cardboard cut-out, figure of one who abandons, neglects, or ignores his vocation. Whatever we think vocation truly is, in him we see it is not about religion (in the political sense he employs it), it is not about power (in the selfish way he deploys it), it is not about possessions (in the greedy way he enjoys them) and it is not about intellect (in the foolish ways he toys with it). All of these pale before the throne of God Almighty, the one who is truly King. We can't outsmart, out possess, or out manoeuvre God, but Ahab seems to believe that kingship is all about him and to be used on his terms for his gain.

Remember that I am describing this as panto (oh no you aren't, oh yes I am). Don't lose this perspective now as we think more carefully about the implications this historical drama for our contemporary lives. This reads like a humorous midrash on Israelite kingship, on Jewish leadership and both the comedy and the teaching are gift. Jewish teachers reflect and argue and tell stories. They debate with narrative. Jewish humour is, well it is humorous. We see this in Jesus' own teaching. This is exactly what is going on in these chapters and we have much to learn. The trick, though, will be to hold the meaning as gently as we hold the story in order that we do not crush the life out of it. God's instruction is sometimes (perhaps even often) like this, it appears fragile and indistinct when we first encounter it, like a dandelion seed that is light enough to blow on the wind, but when it takes root it is more oak than dandelion. Let's join in and discover.

Here are some of the questions about Ahab's approach to vocation that I notice:

Question 1: partners and friends

Ahab's failure of vocation is highlighted in the first moment of meeting him. He does evil and then he takes an enemy as a wife and adopts her gods. Moreover, we have seen how he chooses to return to her time and time again, even when his eyes have been opened to the reality of the LORD and God's Kingship over Israel. In this drama he partners with Jezebel, with the prophets of Baal, the prophets of Asherah (who are only mentioned in passing), with the false prophets he gathers around supposedly in the LORD's name, and when he partners with Jehoshaphat it is only to try to use him. Each successive bad choice of partner simply compounds error upon error and reinforces brokenness.

If we are serious about vocation, we need to attend to who we choose as our friends and partners. Flawed vocation is contagious. We need to ask who shapes our views and demands our attention. We need to be deliberate about those to whom we devote ourselves and note how each small devotion shapes our larger devotion. We are social and relational beings, and vocation (in the sense of that deep call of God in our lives inviting us into a life of specific and devoted service) will always be mediated in the context of the social setting in which we place ourselves. This is not to suggest that God is unable to speak from beyond such a context (he does that all the time), or to challenge such a context (he does that a lot too, in my experience), but simply to observe that, like Ahab, we will process what he says in particular places with particular people and according to certain societal norms or expectations. Those around us, particularly those closest to our hearts, form a kind of lens through which we perceive everything, even God. These can help, sometimes, but Ahab shows very clearly how they can hinder.

We will return in the final chapter to consider how we discern vocation in our own lives. One of the mistakes we can so easily make is to believe we do this by ourselves. You matter, of course, and your role is key, but I dare to suggest that you are blinkered if you think that you are not being influenced by those around you, and I cannot think of any discernment process which fails to attend to the way in which God is speaking through the wider community about a particular vocation. We do this very deliberately when it comes to ordained vocations: it really doesn't matter how much a candidate feels called if it is not recognised by those around them. Indeed, in our ordination service there is a dialogue between the Bishop and the congregation where the Bishop asks if it is the congregation's will that the ordination proceeds, and whether they will uphold and encourage those who are to be ordained.

I often joke at this point in an ordination service that, if I am not persuaded by the answers, we will move straight to the end of the service and grab a coffee. This is no mere rhetorical gag, it is a legal truth: I am not allowed to ordain without congregational assent and support.

This is true in other walks of life. Medics only start training after interviews and examination which, in part, test vocation. Other vocations are tested more brutally. You might have a vocation to be a barman or comedian, but if no-one comes to your bar or your gigs then you might eventually discern you got your sense of calling wrong. We return later to how we might be of support in the church in this way, the point for now is the reverse of this: those who actively oppose God may well not be the best advisors when it comes to reflecting on your own vocation.

If you want to develop Godly vocation: hang out with Godly people!

Question 2: attention

Similarly, it is really clear who Ahab listens to: mainly, of course, to Jezebel. It is she who interprets Elijah's actions on Mount Carmel. It is she who will 'deal with' the vineyard 'problem'. She is the voice whispering in his ear by night and setting the tone by day. More than that, in Chapter 22, Ahab will have a choice as to whom he gives his attention: Jehoshaphat, Micaiah, Zedekiah, 'the prophets', voices offstage like the courtiers, his own self-image, or Jezebel.

This might feel very similar to the previous point, and it certainly overlaps, but it is distinct in the sense that we give attention beyond our social circles and our immediate relationships. We don't know how this worked in Ahab's time, really, but clearly this matters today. In a world of social media, internet search engines, books galore, and all manner of other media, we have a choice about what we give our attention to. This choice is far more powerful than we probably realise.

More than that, though: our world has changed more subtly than we might realise until we stop and think. In the world of Cambridge Analytica (or countless others who mine data and shape social media), we would be wise to reflect on the ways in which our attention is deliberately manipulated by others to their own ends. Most people are aware that algorithms shape what we see on social media, even if we don't really know what that means. I am not an expert, but would observe that this highlights the need to be very deliberate if we want to attend first and foremost to God. I don't want to turn into conspiracy-theorist; there is no need to panic, but there is a real need to employ common sense and apply yourself to making good and deliberate decisions.

Attention tends to be given in a thousand small ways rather than one big one. It is shaped by the habits of thought to which we return, the daydreams we welcome, and the ambitions we foster. It is an inclination of the heart as much as a directing of the mind. It is fostered by repeated small disciplines that point you to the Word, remind you to pray, and develop Christlike character. What habits do you have, or need, to enable you to focus on God? And, conversely, are there those you should be losing?

If you want to develop Godly vocation, find (practical) ways of focussing your attention on God.

Question 3: fruit

It is astonishing to note how blind Ahab is to the fruit of his actions. Of course, this is highlighted in the way the drama plays out on the stage of the scriptures. Time is compressed and expanded (as it is in the telling of any story) with 4 days passing in one verse whilst a few hours take 40 or 50 verses. The author does the hard work of picking out events to highlight and focus our attention, and we would be wise to remember that it would have felt different to live through this than it does to read about it. However, when Ahab listened to Elijah or one of the true prophets things went well, and when he didn't they went wrong...

... except of course that he will end up with that vineyard.

... and beat Ben-hadad.

... and persuade Jehoshaphat to go into battle with him (sorry for the spoilers).

It wasn't such good news for the prophets of Baal on Carmel, but you can't win them all.

Looking at fruit is not a simplistic thing, or even something that is easily defended in the face of a persistent onslaught of opposition. However, we do feel it. This is one of the things that this 'panto' draws out so brilliantly: Ahab becomes a faithless king, a murdering monarch, a self-obsessed tyrant who gives away his wives and kids to save his own skin. He becomes a shadow of decency, and this does not happen without being aware of it. The selfish fruit might appear fulsome, but it comes at the cost of the soul.

Indeed, we will see glimpses of this realisation in his limited self-knowledge and repentance at the end of chapter 21 and in his conversation with Micaiah, but it is not enough to bring him to the point of radical renewal and recalibration of his life.

Vocation must be whole person. If it is of God, it might cost you everything, but it will also bring life in fuller fulness than you will ever have conceived. How do you build in those sense-check mechanisms that allow for course-correction as you see the fruit being borne by the direction of your life?

Moreover, consider the fruit that arose around Ahab. I lose count of the number of people who are murdered, disinherited, or cast out in these passages. The whole kingdom is placed into disarray by the wicked warpedness of a self-centred king and the fruit will be destruction as we are clearly told in the text. It might not come in his lifetime, but it will surely come (as it did). Elijah is sent to the outcast (as we saw in chapter 18) in order that the fruit of his life might be blessing in theirs, Ahab is so blinded by the self-enhancing fruit he desires that he would barely even realise that the poor even exist.

If you want to develop Godly vocation: pay attention to the fruit you are bearing internally and externally.

Question 4: self-orientation

Perhaps the clearest problem with Ahab is that he is utterly obsessed with himself: his wellbeing, his possession, his victory, his glory, his reputation, and so on. This is, perhaps the clearest difference between him and the prophets: for the prophet's life is not primarily about them. One of the most surprising things is that they keep getting replaced before they can become the centre of the story. Elijah, such a hero of history, comes and will shortly go. So will Micaiah. One of the prophets will not even be named. Ahab, though, expects the world to revolved around him. Perhaps my imagination is running wild here, but I am hearing a clever play on the song from 'Hamilton' the musical, portraying King George III dancing on the stage prattling on about the close and loving relationship he has with subjects about whom he cares not at all. 'Let there be drought! Give me your vineyard! Let others die in my place! I am a strategist not a coward! And the king should be well provisioned, after all.'

And, as soon as you read this, you may want to object that I am overlooking proper self-care, which is just as much God's will for us as caring for others. Of course it is, but the problem in this drama, as in much of the Western world today, is what happens when self-care becomes self-obsession. I want more. I deserve better. My rights matter most. The balance is not always easy to strike, but it does need to be struck. Once again, perhaps, this is an area it is hard to get right alone.

This balance of self-care and self-orientation is a really hard one to find when it comes to vocation (and I don't claim I get it right). It is hard, but it is essential. The call of the scriptures is to selfless service; to lay down our lives for the sheep; to take up our cross and follow; to self-denial, love, and service. More, it is shaped by the Bible's teaching that we are to put to death whatever is earthly (including evil desire and greed – see Colossians 3.5).

Ahab is in this gig for himself and that shines through the story. Whatever the tune might be if this story were set to music, the only words you would need to sing along would be 'me me me me meeee'. Not only does this contradict what is required of a king (we shall come back to this in the next section), it is incompatible with any of us following the Living God whom we know now in Christ.

Godly vocation involves huge sacrifice. We need to be careful about imposing a particular interpretation of this sacrifice on others, especially in a one-on-one setting as it is very easy to abuse this. It might be very easy for me to see what I would like you to sacrifice, whilst remaining deaf to that which I am being called to lay down. However, no-one truly follows Christ without experiencing crucifixion so we may not ignore this either. Beware the glittering lights of the successful ministry that seems to offer reward at no cost and be very wary of jealousy. History, theology, and the Bible suggest there may well be more going on than you are allowed to see when vocation only looks like success.

If you want to develop Godly vocation: ask how you get off the throne of your own life.

Question 5: responsibility

Perhaps most importantly, we should note that the fundamental comedy in this pantomime is that Ahab refuses the typology of an Israelite King. Kings were supposed to take after the LORD (who was, is, and always will be the true king) and King David (who was the exemplar king). They were supposed to be just, wise, holy, and generous. They were to be devoted shepherds caring for their flock. They had many privileges but with them came huge responsibility.

Ahab is having none of it. He is not interested in his responsibility, but he is very interested in his privilege. In many ways he is exactly what was promised when Israel asked for a king to start with. It comes to something when Spiderman knows more about Godly leadership than the king of Israel, but Peter Parker (aka Spiderman, of course) is exactly right when he observes that 'with great power comes great responsibility'.

When we ordain people in the Church of England the Bishop reminds each to remember, in Christ's name, the greatness of the trust in which they will share.

(Notice that it is shared. Christ does not just hand over this trust, as if he were dumping it on you and turning his head away to something more interesting. He does not abandon you or the work to which he calls you; he invites you to share.)

The Bishop explains that this is Christ's own servant ministry caring for those who are made in God's image, who are Christ's own flock, and that in serving them the minister serves Christ himself. I always have a sizable lump in my throat at this point in the service.

In so many ways this is true of all vocation, and it was certainly true of Ahab's. The work is God's not ours, and if we cannot grasp this we have not really grasped the vocation at all.

Vocation is not self-serving if it is truly vocation. I suspect that is true in general terms when we think about classic vocations such as medicine or law, but it is certainly true when it comes to all Godly vocation whether the task seems noble or lowly from our perspective. Godly vocation is concerned with shadowing God as he goes about his business, and his concern is the whole flock. Of course he cares for you and will give you a good talking to if you start abusing yourself, but it is not primarily about you. It is about him. And he is about all his children, including you.

George Herbert captures this beautifully in his prayer and hymn: 'Teach me, my God and King, in all things Thee to see, and what I do in anything, to do it as for Thee.' I love both the original and more common words:

> *A servant with this clause,*
> *makes drudgery divine:*
> *who sweeps a room, as for thy laws,*
> *makes that and the action fine.*
>
> *(The original version was:*
>> *If done t'obey Thy laws,*
>> *e'en servile labours shine;*
>> *hallowed is toil, if this the cause,*
>> *the meanest work divine.)*
>
> *This is the famous stone,*
> *that turneth all to gold;*
> *for that which God doth touch and own,*
> *cannot for less be told.*

If you want to develop Godly vocation: pay more attention to your responsibilities than your rights, for in serving others you will find yourself serving God himself.

Question 6: rights

We should also attend to the missing piece in this jigsaw of Ahab's life and our discussion. King David was famously (and faithfully) challenged by the prophet Nathan when he got things wrong (see 2 Samuel 12 for the story). Where, though, is David's Nathan in Ahab's life? Throughout this drama he seems to reject all possible candidates, and one of them was ELIJAH for goodness' sake!

Self-care really does matter in vocation and forgive me if I appear to have downplayed it heretofore. It's just that self-care rarely looks like the world makes it look.

Ahab has all manner of rights as king of Israel. He has the right to have trusted advisors teaching him God's way and God's word. He rejects these. He has the right to worship, and possibly even to preferential attention to his prayers. He despises this, preferring Baal and Asherah. He has the right to repent when he gets it wrong, the right to learn, and develop, and grow. No-one expects perfection (they certainly didn't get it from David).

Ahab appears, though, to throw these rights away and invent his own, and then live in fear that he is going to lose the rights that should never really have been rights to start with. Fear is a really telling emotion. Persistent fear often seems to flag up that we are loosening our grip on Christ's hand, and noticing this can be really helpful. Please don't mishear me; I am not saying that fear is bad in itself, merely that it should be attended to. We noted earlier how Elijah and Obadiah saw it, responded, and chose to trust. Fear can be very natural and can often be good and should be heeded. It usually indicates something is awry, though, and a response is often needed. Moreover, in responding we have a choice about whether our fear pushes us closer to

Christ or drives us away. Ahab repeatedly makes the wrong choice.

Self-care when it comes to Godly vocation is complex. It involves huge amounts of humility and a massive willingness to learn as you follow One who not only knows you better than you know yourself, but also loves you more than you can ever love yourself.

If you want to develop Godly vocation: be willing to learn more about yourself than you ever knew you needed to know.

Question 7:
bitter sullenness and other internal dynamics

We must not forget to reflect on the internal dynamics of vocation. In this question and the next we will think of two such elements (and there are many more). In the coming acts of this panto, we will notice a repeated phrase used to describe Ahab. The phrase appears at the end of Chapter 20 and the beginning of Chapter 21 and seems to open Ahab up to abandoning his vocation for want of a vineyard. He will become 'resentful and sullen', a comic expression appearing on the face of a king in a pantomime setting, but a serious condition in real life. Perhaps it is not surprising that it will be a phrase that is repeated, both to play to the audience and to emphasise the import of what is going on.

Throughout, Ahab does not seem to attend at all to the internal dynamics raging in his heart, mind, and soul, and this leads to disaster. It will be blindingly obvious to the audience that the King should not be bitter or sullen, but that which is obvious to others is often completely hidden to the one who is wrestling with it.

There are a myriad of reasons why neither resentment nor sullenness make any sense. By the time we get to those words, he will have been delivered from a foreign army. He will repeatedly have heard God's word and been given the chance to repent. He is a king, secure (for now) and still wealthy. He is blind to this, though, because he feels he has been belittled.

If we are wise, we will learn to attend to our own inner warning signs. For myself, when I am stressed I tend to get a mouth ulcer, and I have learned to notice and respond to the stress, not just to the oral discomfort. I try to attend to physical and psychological warning signs in myself and those around me before they become a problem. Indeed, more than that, I try to let them become a blessing by responding early and being open to God's grace and teaching when stuff is hard.

Here are some of the warning signs I see around me:

- What do you do when you notice that you are always rushing your prayers?

- What do you do when you notice that you are in constant conflict with those who have proper authority around you?
- What do you do when you notice you are comfort eating/drinking/watching in an excessive way?
- What do you do with infatuation or compulsion?
- What do you do when you can't sleep, or want to sleep all the time?
- What do you do when your humour is cynical or destructive?
- What do you do when fantasy is more pleasing than reality?

How do you attend to your internal dynamics? What are your key questions?

Another surprising thing about this in the text is that no-one reminds Ahab of how good he has it. Vocation is a privilege and when we forget that we do begin to lose our grip. Archbishop Justin Welby took part in a series of programmes on BBC Radio 4 called 'The Archbishop Interviews', in which he talked to various interesting people about life and faith. One of the most fascinating is when he talks to Tony Blair. They begin to talk about how to cope when people criticise you, and one of them says to the other: 'The thing I always remember is that I get to do this... I get to be Prime Minister... I get to be Archbishop of Canterbury and that is an extraordinary privilege.' It is a beautiful moment of radio, and worth listening to.

The old advice around counting blessings matters when it comes to vocational faithfulness. It can be hard, but it is a privilege... and it is one that Ahab lost all too soon through not seeing this.

If you want to develop Godly vocation: attend with care to what is happening inside you as well as around you. Do not be afraid to seek help.

Question 8: joy (or at least contentment)

The converse of this last observation is also true: one of the marked features of Ahab's life is its apparent joylessness. It is in sharp contrast to the playfulness that we see in Elijah on Carmel or in Micaiah as he stands in front of the court and stands out on the pantomime stage. In Ahab we see a man who seems to have everything, but to enjoy nothing.

This is notably different from the joyful pictures of ordinations that we see each year in the church, or the exuberant celebrations as people qualify as nurses or get a new job. It stands distinct from the holy wonder at the birth of a child and the stepping into a vocation of parenthood. Ahab lacks the satisfaction experienced in a job well done in any walk of life. I have mentioned the question of contentment in vocation before (page 37); it does not seem realistic to me to suggest that vocation is always a barrel of laughs. The Bible does, though, talk both of joy and contentment as marks of the Kingdom of God, and there are clearly serious questions to be considered when they are completely absent.

We need to be especially careful with this one, though, as I somewhat fear we live in an age which idolises happiness. Joylessness is a warning light, it is a beeping alarm, but it is not a universal sign with only one meaning. It might mean that you have missed or forsaken your vocation, but equally it could mean that you are facing really tough circumstances and need to seek special grace and particular strength and wisdom. It almost always acts as an invitation to return to the Lord in all his kindness. Prayer, patience, perspective, and the advice of wise friends are really important at times like these.

It is certainly true that, when we chase things that are not God's vocation in our lives, we find that we are devoting ourselves to glittering but unsatisfying prizes. Vocation is altogether more substantial, more filling, more joyful, more holy, and more worthwhile. Equally, we would not be being true to the gospel call of Christ if we failed to note that the call to follow is a call to take up our cross, an invitation to join the apostle as he testifies 'I have been crucified, and I live, no longer I, but Christ lives in me' (from Gal 2.19-20).

That being said, we should not despise happiness. God is very kind and often places us in good places. I got a text from a friend the other day who was really happy to have got back to work after a few days away; they seemed to suggest they might be odd to enjoy their role. It didn't take much for me to reply saying that it was not odd at all, simply a beautiful sign of God's kindness that they were both blessed and a blessing in their calling. I think it was their reply that makes me recall the conversation: 'Wow – what a way to start the day! He is so very good.' I suspect God delights when we are happy, it is just that this is not the be all and end all.

If you want to develop Godly vocation: remember if you pursue happiness, you will lose it like a child trying to capture newly blown bubbles. Pursue God and his call on your life, you will find a deep contentment and much joy, costly though it may be at times.

Question 9: boundaries

Finally, the other main difference I notice between Ahab and the prophets is how they observe boundaries. Jesus, himself, observes that there were many widows around during the drought, indeed that there were widows in Israel at the time, but Elijah only goes to the one to whom he is sent. He cannot and must not do everything.

Ahab, by contrast, cannot control himself. He sees, he wants, he takes. He will wage battle as and when he chooses. He has no sense of his boundedness.

I don't know that I need to observe much more about this question. If you want to develop Godly vocation: pay attention to the fact that it is as much about what we don't do as what we do do. It is limited, focussed, and sometimes 'less really is more'.

And so, back to the drama...

7. PANTO ACT 4:

QUESTIONS OF COWARDICE,
SALVATION, AND OBEDIENCE
(1 KINGS 20)

Up goes the curtain! The scenery has changed again and we come to an oft-forgotten act in the middle of this pantomime. In reality it is the first of three 'set pieces' which comprise the final three acts of this panto and result in the (un)timely death of Ahab. We will scamper through them, enjoying the similar shape and trying not to wince as the foolish king fails to 'get' the increasingly obvious point. Drama, prophecy, intervention, disobedience, and judgement are the recipes of the second half of this panto.

This set-piece involves 34 kings (Ben-hadad of Aram, 32 Allied kings, and Ahab) several battles, at least one hundred and thirty five thousand soldiers, and a couple of prophets. There is much sound and fury on stage, but the point is very simple really. The action goes on, but it's a bit like one of those Marvel films where the plot is basically 'loads of bad guys, everything should go wrong, there is interminable fighting, noise, and special effects... but look! Da dah! Someone happens just to have the right super-power to save the day', and you walk out the cinema knowing that is two hours you won't get back. This panto is more my taste, but I might just fast-forward a bit if you don't mind too much.

So, let's cut to the chase:

- King Ben-hadad of Aram (baddy) gathers 32 royal chums and a huge army and marches against Samaria, capital city of Israel where Ahab is king. (v1)
- He lays siege and attacks. He demands all Ahab's silver, gold, fairest children, and fairest wives. (Interestingly this does not appear to include Jezebel as she will reappear next chapter: we are still in panto, and in this production Jezebel is anything but fair... in any sense of that word.) (vv2-3)
- Ahab hands them over. (v4)
- Ben-hadad does not believe Ahab has done as he demanded so says he will send the domestic or marital inspectors in. Interestingly, this is the point at which Ahab kicks off, he is willing to give up his

treasure and family but doubting his honesty is one step too far. We are spoiling for a conflict. (vv5-12)

- An unnamed prophet bobs up promising victory, so Ahab musters his feeble troops, rides out and defeats the Arameans. Round 1 to God and Ahab, and the prophet comes back and encourages Ahab. (vv13-22)
- The Arameans regroup and reattack in the spring with a massive army. The Israelites are like two 'flocks of goats', but God grants victory both on the battlefield and through a collapsing wall. Once again, he does this so that Ahab may 'know he is the LORD'. (vv23-30)
- Ben-hadad hides in the city and Ahab is merciful to him for political and territorial gain. (vv30-34)
- Finally (almost), the prophets condemn Ahab because, even though God has given victory, Ahab has tried to bring his own advantage by not carrying out the judgement of God on Ben-hadad. (vv35-42)
- And in the dying moments of the act we see Ahab walking home alone and get a glimpse into his heart. He appears to feel he is owed but he hasn't got the credit he deserves. This is nonsense, of course, but that makes no difference in pantomime. Ahab is resentful. He is sullen. And the next act will explore what this looks like. (v43)

This act is dramatic, but the point is simple: there is hope when Ahab listens to the prophets (and thus to God) and none when he doesn't. God does not give up trying to rescue him, but the inner battle is far more fierce than the outer one. The king cannot learn, and he ends up resenting what God has done and all those who are meant to be gifts of grace to him.

Notice this, please: the inner life really matters when it comes to vocation. You can't grow good fruit in impoverished, dry, stony, overgrown, or poisoned soil (someone ought to tell a story about that...).

8. PANTO ACT 5:
NABOTH'S VINEYARD,
ELIJAH'S SWAN-SONG, AND
A GLIMMER OF HOPE (1 KINGS 21)

In some ways 1 Kings 21 has a similar shape to chapters 20 and 22. The action, prophecy, hope, and judgement cycle is familiar, but each act brings new insight and fresh surprise. There are three scenes about to unfold before us and they are of a completely different scale to the preceding chapter.

Scene 1 (vv1-16)

As the curtain parts we are longer find ourselves surrounded by the vast sweep of battlefields and armies, but alone in a summer palace with Ahab and Jezebel. The text is deliberately vague about timing and how we got here (which may be another indication that this is narrative to be enjoyed and not merely studied). We are in Jezreel rather than Samaria. Jezreel was strategically important, but Samaria was the capital and we have seen last chapter that Ahab and his families were also based there for at least some of the time. It could be that they have left because of the fighting and damage, but this is not the point of the story. Ahab is not concerned with affairs of state, he is pining after a bit of real estate.

A man called Naboth owns a vineyard next to the palace. Ahab wants it to grow vegetables (v2). There may be some comic irony and deliberate wider biblical echoing here in that Israel is often likened to God's vine (see Isaiah 5 for example) and here is Ahab wanting to change the purpose of this land from vineyard to veggie plot. The main point, though, is that Naboth is not interested in selling up, either for cash or for better land. He feels so strongly that he invokes the LORD as the one who forbids (v3) which is weighty stuff for a Jew of any era.

Ahab, for the second time in 5 verses, is resentful and sullen. Don't miss the comedy of the mardy king who gets such a sulk on that he will not even eat. This is the ultimate 'spoiled child having a strop' moment. It is, though, fascinating that this is the way that he's described. Even though God is doing great things around him, Ahab is resentful and sullen because he doesn't get the glory for defeating the Aramaeans. Even though he has a palace, he's resentful and sullen because he can't have Naboth's vineyard. What is true on the public and geopolitical level is replicated and reflected on the personal level. Vocation is not only, indeed perhaps not mainly and certainly not primarily, concerned with the big picture stuff, it is about the inner walk of one whom today we might call a disciple.

Right on cue: in comes Jezebel (boo, hiss, don't pretend that you have not missed her). She gives Ahab a proper talking to and then takes matters into her own hands, redefining kingship as she does so. The King of Israel is meant to be a shepherd, to cherish and care for the people and to ensure justice is done. Jezebel orchestrates a feast, pretending to be Ahab, and arranges for Naboth to be murdered. The scene is bloody and seems designed to be almost deliciously wicked in order that we might revel unrestrained in our hatred for the wicked queen. As with all good theatre, in this moment we can suspend reality, ignore the complexity of real life and give ourselves over the simplicity of the plot and the emotion it evokes. Forget your own inner Jezebel for a moment and live the loathing... you will never confront your own demons if you do not glimpse how bad they really are.

Ahab hears about this and moves into the vineyard.

Once again, please pause and note two vital things which would be easy but disastrous to miss. We miss the point if we either blame Jezebel for Ahab's actions or fail to observe her impact on us. She is a deliberate 'given' in the text. She is, of course, a historical character but in this production she is being used by the narrator to make a point. She is the snake of Genesis 3 or the Haman of Queen Esther's court. She is not wicked because she is female or foreign, although the story sadly does play on those stereotypes in the audience's mind; she is a necessary character and the actual focus is on Ahab... and (because this is the Bible and not really pantomime) on the audience.

Thus, the first thing we might miss is the intended impact of the multilevel effect of pantomime. In the moment in this auditorium we are meant to 'enjoy' the wickedness of Jezebel (in the sense that 'baddies' are meant to be enjoyable on stage), but at the same time we should find ourselves deeply uncomfortable at the way we, too, write off others based on difference. In this narrative we see racism and sexism at work, at the very least in the way the story has been portrayed over the years. For ourselves, we may or may not wrestle with one or both of those specific sins, but I have yet to meet someone who is not tempted to write off some types of people. 'Othering' those who are different to us sometimes seems almost as human as breathing. As with the best comedy, this should make us laugh and wince in the same moment. It should lower our defences in order that we might examine our own lives in an undefended manner. Amusement, even enjoyment, should lead to observation, remorse, and reshaping of life, for in so engaging we find we have heard the prophetic call of God that Ahab so tragically misses.

Secondly, though, please don't let Ahab off the hook. Jezebel is a reality in his life, but he is a morally independent actor. He can be broken or woken by her, unmade or remade, putrefied or purified, just as each of us can by temptation. He chooses to listen, to follow, to take advantage, and to school his heart after her image. It might be love that makes him act as he does, it might be lust, or weakness, or envy, or pride. It could be the apparently simple lure of politics, but it is unholy and unwise, and it blinds and deafens him to the gracious call of the God who does not give up.

Scene 2 (vv17-24)

Talking of which, along comes Elijah, at God's instruction, for his final moment on stage in this drama and this book, actually. It might surprise you to notice that he only appears in the chapters we have explored and then briefly in the first couple of chapters of 2 Kings: his impact in the biblical narrative feels much bigger than this. (Glancing down at the programme you may or may not have bought on the door you will see that Elijah is named 37 times in 1 Kings, 21 times in 2 Kings, gets one passing mention in 2 Chronicles, and only appears once in the minor prophets. He is referenced 5 times in the intertestamental literature (or Apocrypha) and 29 times in the New Testament.)

We, in the audience, get treated to a bit of off-stage dialogue between God and Elijah as God specifies very precisely which Ahab we are discussing (v18) as if Elijah might not know. In our own aside it is always worth remembering that the things that matter most on the stage of our little panto are not always as momentous in God's eternity.

The LORD blames Ahab directly for the killing of Naboth (I told you that it was his fault not Jezebel's! I whispered that to you before, when it happened. I know you will never want to sit next to me again at the Panto, but it's nice to be right sometimes.) Then he says that dogs will lick up Ahab's blood in the same spot Naboth was stoned and bled to death. Again, what an astonishingly gory we are presented with! And for the original audience, how doubly horrid: they hated dogs then almost as much as most of us love them today.

Hang on though! It gets better, both in bloody detail and then in a final shocking twist of grace. Elijah condemns Ahab because he has made God angry and provoked Israel to sin (v22). Even better (in the moral framework of the pantomime, at least), Jezebel shall be eaten by those loathsome dogs and so will anyone belonging to Ahab in the city.

In many ways, apart from the actual dying, this should be the end of the panto, except that God really doesn't give up.

Scene 3 (vv25-29)

Scene 3 feels like it is going to be the 'dagger in the heart' scene. Listen to the opening words:

Indeed, there was no one like Ahab, who sold himself to do what was evil in the sight of the LORD, urged on by his wife Jezebel. He acted most abominably in going after idols, as the Amorites had done, whom the LORD drove out before the Israelites. (vv25-26)

We have seen the direction of travel, it has been repeated, and we know what is happening... until we get to verse 27. Ahab hears and repents, and God promises mercy.

Hang on, don't ruin the story, I was enjoying that!

No, wait, this is what we want to happen. We like repentance, and mercy, and lives being put back together. Sorry, we were getting carried away.

Finally!

Ahab listens, responds, and God relents. We should not get overly bothered by the apparent delay in judgement, the pattern of the Bible is that God always responds to humility and obedience. Ahab is humble, and even now God's grace is sufficient and his heart is big enough to stay his hand of judgement.

We are on the edge of our seats awaiting the final act! What will happen? Patience, friend! First comes a comfort break and a bit of refreshment.

9. VOCATION EMBRACED:
ENGAGING ELIJAH
AND THE OTHER PROPHETS

Before the final act, the final interval: let's return to our conversation as the scenery is changed. It is good and proper that we learn from Ahab's errors, and the text seems to be written to allow us to do exactly that. It is often said that a sensible person learns from their own mistakes and a wise person also learns from other people's.

Ahab's is not the only gift on offer here, though, there is a sunny side to this exploration and it is expressed through the prophets in the text. We have seen that their calling is often hard, always real, and occasionally uncomfortable, but it is also fruitful, engaged, and persistent. It is about others not just them, and they have much to teach us about vocation if we are serious about listening, learning, and experimenting.

If Ahab raises questions for us to wrestle with as we explore vocation today, it seems to me that the prophets open invitations from the LORD's heart to ours; invitations that start on paper but lead to encounter and relationship; invitations that can be captured in a few words that lead to a life beyond any description; invitations which many receive but all must encounter personally.

Invitation 1: obedience (and trust)

The first, and perhaps the most obvious insight the prophets offer into vocation is that it is steeped in obedience to God. The LORD, at least in these events, often seems to give counterintuitive instructions, and the prophets are a blessing (and are often blessed) when they follow them.

Elijah starts off by leaving the nation of Israel and cohabiting with a foreign widow!

Micaiah, as we are about to witness, tells Ahab a lie because the king is not interested in the truth!

The prophets listen, follow, and obey, and in so doing they enable God's word to be heard even if it is not followed by others.

I am not sure we are very good at obedience in our generation (if we ever were). I shall return to this below, but it seems to me that we can be pretty much guaranteed to want to do something if we are told not to. Some years ago, one Sunday morning, I stuck a prominent sign outside a storeroom door at the back of the church where I was then Vicar. You couldn't miss it when you walked into church. It said 'No entry! By order of the Vicar and Church Wardens' and had a no-entry road sign drawn on it in bright red. I sat in my Vicar's seat and watched what happened. Some came in talking and didn't see it. A few noticed and clearly asked about it. But many of the 'leading members' of church peered through the door to see what was new in there. I mentioned this in the sermon (I know I am horrible, and I can't even remember exactly what I was preaching on) to much hilarity and embarrassment, but the point stood then as it would stand now. We are not good at obedience.

Obedience, you see, requires both trust and humility, and these are hard. We will return to humility in a moment, but we do need to note the link between trust and obedience when it comes to God because it works differently to how it would with a human. You might trust me completely, but usually that would not lead to you obeying me (and it would be a bit weird if that were either your or my expectation). Sometimes it would: if, for example you faced a life-threatening situation and I commanded you to take a particular action. "Get out of the way of the bus!" "Don't drink that, it's poisonous!". However, God is different to me (in so many ways). He is not another human being, fallible, weak, and limited as you and I are. Trusting him does not only mean that you believe what he says, but that you place yourself in his hands. Obedience is part of discipleship, even though it is hard to pin down.

Godly vocation is, I think, a bit like stage-diving. I have never done it, I am sad to say, but when someone launches off a stage people either catch them or they plummet nose-first to a grubby floor. If I may be so direct, I would suggest that your vocation is either utterly in God's hands or you still have something to learn about how God wants to partner with you in changing the world. This is not really a surprise, as vocation that follows Christ must be about faith. The word we translate as 'faith' we also translate as 'belief' or 'trust'; it means full confidence and trust which will be lived out. It is the kind of trust you place in a chair when you lower your weight into it, or into a friend who offers you a piggy-back or to fix your precious broken cup. Vocation usually involves this kind of leap of faith. (Moreover, talking of grubby floors, don't be surprised when it leads you to unclean places and broken people; Jesus has an especial fondness for those that the world overlooks.)

Trust, and the consequent obedience, takes determination, repetition, and practice. It is hard at any time, but perhaps particularly today.

Vocation really does require trusting obedience to God's call.

Invitation 2:
being real – part one: the gritty reality

Equally obviously, as far as I can see, the prophets don't get it easy. Clearly Elijah feels this: do you remember his words from Chapter 19: 'It is enough; now, O LORD, take away my life, for I am no better than my ancestors'? Look out for the way Micaiah gets stuck in prison on reduced rations of bread and water? And recall how Obadiah is terrified that Ahab might find him out?

The prophet's life is not an easy one full of obvious blessing, fun, and frivolity. It is tough, real, and demanding, and it is usually in this place that they find God and share him with others. Vocation is not for wimps, it is not romantic, and in my experience it is far from easy.

Think about Elijah in most of his journey from Horeb to Moriah. We have no idea how he knows where to go. We don't hear any real details of his journey, in fact the text seems deliberately marked with silence. All we know is that God has fed him and will meet him (he doesn't even know the latter for certain, of course). He just plods on, putting one foot in front of the other, doing the only thing that makes sense to him in the moment. We hear a great deal of detail about the few hours spent on Mount Moriah, and quite a bit about the few minutes' worth of drama on Mount Horeb, but nothing at all about the month and half journeying across the desert. How do you imagine vocation felt to Elijah?

This is a vital question for our movie-moulded imaginations to live with, wrestle with, and maybe eventually grasp. Vocation sounds so impressive and looks great on Netflix. In reality, though it often feels like I imagine it felt to Elijah; it is worked out in patience over a long period of time. The soul is tested and formed not so much in dramatic acts of wonder, but faithful ongoing acts of service. It might be symbolic, iconic, and almost glamourous in the public gaze, but it is held in a daily grappling with the reality of our own and others' pain and fostered in gritty love before the throne of grace. Vocation is tough, real, determined, and sometimes very painful indeed. But it changes everything. Vocation is always worked out in the real world never in some kind of spiritual fantasy world.

This is why we hold it together with the need to learn to be kind to ourselves as well as others. God does not regard you as a disposable commodity, and you are still human. Take time off! Discover how to have fun! Make friends! (I could go on, but you have probably got the point.)

Vocation engages with the gritty reality of life.

Invitation 3:
being real – part two: warts and all

This theme of real-ness, which somehow feels a more apt description than 'reality', is not just observing that life can be hard and vocation serves the tough stuff... not least because life is not always hard, it's not hard for everyone, and it is not hard all the time. Imagine what it would feel like to 'play' Elijah in this drama if it were really acted out on stage. You would have a ball, and laugh as much as you cried. Can you taste the sweet thrill of proving all those prophets wrong? Do you imagine he and the widow did not make friends? Have you ever tasted God's cooking, even alone in a deserted place? Above all, can you imagine the peace of meeting the LORD in utter silence?

As you watch this drama and think about the reality of living through it, do you imagine that Elijah (or any of the other prophets) really got everything right? Of course it looks like they did on stage, although apparently some people argue that the showdown on Carmel was done without God's instruction. I don't really agree, it would run counter to the flow of the text, I think, but even so I have argued that we see Elijah's failure at the start of 1 Kings 19 (the very next chapter in the biblical text). Vocation does not just wave a magic wand and deal with the reality of the world around us, it does so by engaging the whole reality of who we are. One of the most perplexing, but liberating, things about the Bible is that we repeatedly see God bringing his plans to bear even when those who follow things get things muddled, wrong, or broken. Whether we think of Elijah, Jonah, Peter, or Saul/Paul, God has a remarkable way of weaving our foolishness into his grace.

The pressure to be perfect is immense today. It is exacerbated by social media and reinforced by the easy way in which we judge other people. It leads to very real problems when people realise it is easier to pretend to be good than actually to be good (and we come back to this in a moment), but it also denies God the ability to work in our imperfection.

I love the passage in 2 Corinthians 12 where Paul is driven to explain how he is weakened by a 'thorn in his flesh', which I think we often take as meaning an external irritation but I read as being part of him, or at least as being a way to explore a part of him before God. The metaphor of a thorn suggests externality: human flesh is not normally adorned with thorns and they hurt when they stick in. Moreover, the 'thorn' is described as a 'messenger of Satan'. Indeed, Paul's threefold request that it would 'leave' (the word also means desist, fall away, or refrain) seems to imply that he sees this as something beyond himself which is in some manner oppressing him.

However, something changes when God speaks. He says, 'My grace is sufficient for you, for power is made perfect in weakness.' His grace abounds, and it finds its workshop, its gallery, its springboard in your weakness.

Paul responds by choosing to boast in weakness. He has learned (as must we) not to blame circumstances or others for his stumblings, but rather to offer his brokenness as part of himself to God. It doesn't matter what the cause is, in one way, the weakness is tied up with who he now is and that is the only gift he can offer God. Paul has glimpsed that we cannot sort ourselves out before we offer to serve. We can only come as we are.

When I was 15 or 16, I responded to the minister's call to come forward and be prepared for baptism (I grew up in the Baptist Church). I was sitting with my friends and the last thing I wanted to do was look foolish, far less well up with tears, but we started singing and suddenly vocation made sense... it really isn't about achievement, or ability, or even effort (although there will be lots of effort), it's about whole-person availability. This is what we sang:

> *Just as I am, without one plea,*
> *but that thy blood was shed for me,*
> *and that thou bidd'st me come to thee,*
> *O Lamb of God, I come.*
>
> *Just as I am, and waiting not*
> *to rid my soul of one dark blot,*
> *to thee, whose blood can cleanse each spot,*
> *O Lamb of God, I come.*
>
> *Just as I am, though tossed about*
> *with many a conflict, many a doubt,*
> *fightings and fears within, without,*
> *O Lamb of God, I come.*
>
> *Just as I am, poor, wretched, blind;*
> *Sight, riches, healing of the mind;*
> *Yes, all I need, in Thee to find,*
> *O Lamb of God, I come!*
>
> *Just as I am, thou wilt receive,*
> *wilt welcome, pardon, cleanse, relieve;*

> *because thy promise I believe,*
> *O Lamb of God, I come.*
>
> *Just as I am, Thy love unknown*
> *Has broken every barrier down;*
> *Now, to be Thine, yea, Thine alone,*
> *O Lamb of God, I come!*
>
> *(Charlotte Elliot (1789-1871))*

Vocation takes the whole reality of what you do and who you are, with all your success and failure, and engages it all in the service of God.

Invitation 4:
being real – part three: transparency and integrity

This hymn takes us to a third really important aspect to being real. We have noted that vocation engages the whole reality of the lives of those we serve. It does so despite our imperfections, indeed often working with those apparent flaws and mistakes; we do not need to pretend. God chooses to send flawed servants (like you and me) to a broken world, not to be saviours but to be witnesses, not to be heroes but to carry a message of hope, not to be perfect but to be examples. This ministry, whatever our vocation, must be firmly embodied in a whole life transparently, wholeheartedly, and completely given over to Christ.

In a world where we glimpse each other at our best and in passing, where we seem to set out to perform and get slated if we confess our weakness, it is so easy to pretend. In reality, I may be quite good at stuff but I am far from the finished article, yet often it is easiest to pretend either to be hopeless or perfect. It is simpler, for example, either to fake being thick-skinned or give up completely than it is to deal with being hurt. It is easy either to play ignorant or to stay quiet and pretend you know stuff, because engaging in a learning process takes effort. It is nice when you can avoid getting the blame for stuff (even if it is your fault it happened in the first place) but sometimes it is simplest to take the blame for everything. No one really needs me to trail my ignorance, rehearse my insecurities, or seek affirmation all the time... or conversely to claim to be a genius, pretend invulnerability, or suggest I have no need of others... but it can be a small step from common sense in such matters into complete pretence one way or another.

It is profoundly challenging to occupy well the middle space between perfection and uselessness. Do not underestimate the humility, vulnerability, and challenge of living a life which carries significant gifts but is as yet unfinished as you live out your vocation. I had the privilege of serving for a year as a student alongside Simon Walker who later wrote 'The Undefended Leader'. I recommend it highly as an excellent read, but if I were to describe its value in a sentence it would be the way he spells out the need for the 'frontstage' of our lives (the bit everyone sees) to be in step with the 'backstage' of our lives (the private stuff behind the scenery and curtains).

We live in an age which has discovered afresh the value of authenticity (at least in so far as we expect it in others). Transparency is a highly prized characteristic in leaders and in leadership structures. In truth, neither you nor I are never going to be perfect this side of the LORD's return. We should always (in some ways) strive to be as we co-operate with the LORD's forgiveness, power, and grace. However, if we pretend to be the finished article, the best outcome will be that we get found out (the worse one might be that others start believing us, but perhaps the worst is when we start believing it). I described the second part of the invitation to reality to be a call to offer all that we are, but it is a further step of humble obedience to live this call transparently. Ironically, though, when we do live with such transparency we discover that God is able to use our imperfection, just as he used Paul's, to minister to other equally imperfect people around us.

In this drama we get the narrator's view, of course, which sees everything needed for the story. We see Elijah, particularly Elijah, at his best and worst, but have little idea how he lived that out. I suspect this is different for each person and in each vocation, and that Spiritual disciplines appropriate to your vocation are vital. I often joke that I am fed up, as a bishop, of being either deified or demonised each time I walk into a room. When I have to make a decision, you might like what I decide or hate it, but you can be assured that the 'inner Mark' will have usually done his very best in deciding (even if it turns out later that he was wrong). Finding ways to stay patently real, whilst inhabiting the weirdness that is being a bishop of the Church of England in the twenty-first century, is essential for the state of my soul as well as the ministry I am able to offer.

The 1 Kings text we have been considering is really clear, both positively and negatively, that vocation is at least as much about what happens in your heart as it is about what you do. Vocation is fundamentally about what we might now call your own discipleship rather than being about your activity or skillset. It concerns character far more than it does competence. It is vital that we grasp this if we are to avoid becoming fake Christian versions of the 'Ring-wraiths' in Lord of the Rings. It is dangerously easy to become hollow shadows of those who behave right and look impressive on the outside, but have become rotten and empty inside.

In ordination-training circles we often teach that ordained vocation only arises out of baptismal vocation, and will always rest on it. What we mean is that you are first and foremost a baptised follower of Jesus Christ and it is only within this identity and calling that people are called to ordination. Lose the childlike faith that roots us in Christ and we have lost all that we are and have no other vocation in him.

There are real questions here about how we hold all this in whatever context we might find ourselves. I can't imagine the pressures that some of my sister and brother Christians face: the palliative-care nurse with a grieving family, the teacher longing to care but lacking resource, the refuse-collector sitting in the truck cab with co-workers telling jokes that are filthy but still funny, or the teenager pressured into certain online groups. We will live this part of our call differently, but we will face similar basic questions and can support each other. I don't have easy answers, and often feel that I learn more by getting stuff wrong than by getting it right, but holding on to the question really matters.

Vocation is not an act, a job, or a role. Of course, there will be times when we shape our approach to better serve others, but vocation is at least as much about who we are as what we do.

Invitation 5: humility

In this call to reality we have already begun to glimpse that humility is vital. If you come to Christ expecting to discover you are a super-hero, please think again. You will find that you are more loved than you can possibly imagine, but you will also come to see yourself more clearly than you ever have before.

I don't mean that people will criticise you, although they probably will. (Always remember that criticism says at least as much about the critic as it does about you, not least because they almost certainly will not notice this.)

Neither do I mean that God will set you up to fail; he won't (I can't speak for anyone else, but I make enough mistakes without his help). He will, though, use your failures to work acts of grace and love if you are willing to let him.

I mean that as you begin to trust that he really loves you and will never stop doing so, that he chooses to trust you, and that he delights to work in and through you; as you sit in that place and begin to see yourself without the pressure of needing to prove yourself, you will begin to realise that you are not quite the finished article.

Let me switch to the first-person because I can say things about myself that I would never dream of saying about others. When I look at myself reflected in Jesus' eyes I begin to glimpse what an adored wally I really am. I have no idea why he loves me so much when he knows so completely what a foolish muppet I am, but he does. And my calling is to be a trusting, loving, obedient, willing idiot in his service. This is my highest calling and there is such freedom here.

Humility doesn't mean pretending I am not good at some things, or that I get nothing right. It means that I still have so much to learn. It is the freedom not to need to be first violin even though it is hard when I am passed by, or get chosen for the basketball team even though I would love to have played, because I get to play alongside Jesus... and fascinatingly that makes me a far better first-violinist when I get to give that a bash. Humility is playful, joyful, inquisitive, and attentive liberty which is life-giving to the humble and the served.

Humility certainly doesn't mean thinking badly of yourself, putting yourself down, or letting others abuse you. It is not self-condemning, although it can be self-denying. It is not insecure, in fact it is quite the reverse: it requires enough security and maturity to laugh at yourself, learn, and move on. It is sometimes discovered in the 'utter-numpty' moments when we look our foolishness in the face, but just as often explored when we have done really well but hunger to do better, or realise that we were doing things for ourselves and not really for God.

We don't always give the right impression of this in the church, I freely confess. Bishops, indeed clergy in general, are given the best seats and dressed in fancy finery. People stand up when we walk in and listen respectfully even if we drone on and on in the sermon. Looking at the passage again, how do you learn humility as a king? Or as a prophet? How can you be humble without negating your responsibility or refusing to take on that task that God has given to you? I am not going to pretend this is an easy balance, but it is one that matters, which is why we need to practise every day of our lives, and the earlier we start the better!

I do have two 'top tips' viz a viz this, lest it helps: micro-disciplines and playfulness. 'Micro-disciplines' are, at least in my vocabulary, those little repeated things that we do to foster a particular attitude, approach, disposition, or development. I discuss this more fully in *Dancing with Powerlessness* (due out in late 2023, also from *Little House in*

Joppa), but one example for me is that I offer to make drinks in the office when I want one; all too often people bring them to me and it would be so easy to think that was normal. Repeated little invisible disciplines often form the soul more fully than infrequent big acts done for an appreciative audience.

Playfulness is that part of us that spots the ridiculous and is willing to laugh at it... even (perhaps especially) if the ridiculous in question is actually you. Playfulness does not have to be irreverent, disrespectful, dismissive, or unkind. It is warm, human, and real. It spots the absurd with loving appreciation and revels in reality.

You will have other, probably better, techniques to foster humility, but however you do it, it is essential to truly Christian vocation.

Invitation 6: hunger for God

This kind of vulnerable, humble vocation can only be sustained by the kind of hunger for God that we see in Elijah as he treks across the wilderness in his time of greatest weakness. It is not his failure that keeps him going, but his hunger. His vocation comes from God, and the only place he knows where to run is back to God.

It is really striking that 1 Kings 18 and 19 sees Elijah on two different mountain tops. The first is dramatic, loud, popular, and full of 'wow'. The second is silent, alone, and fearful. It is the second that changes his life and the future course of his nation. The place of intimacy always trumps the place of power when it comes to vocation before God.

I hear the Archbishop of York speak regularly, which is a gift I gladly receive. One of the themes to which he keeps returning at the moment, is his concern about the number of clergy who have 'stopped saying their prayers'. The phrase is his, not mine, but I understand what he means by it. It matters because the core of any Christian vocation is our relationship with God.

If my language doesn't work for you, please work out your own translation of it in order that you might hear what I'm saying: the very centre of your vocation is intimacy with God.

It is intimacy in the place of prayer.

It is in the reception of the Holy Eucharist.

It is in the dance of praise.

It is in the washing of people's feet.

It is in the opening of the scriptures and basking in all their wonder.

It is the meeting with Christ in that way that unexpectedly presses pause on the universe and enables things to make sense even just for a fraction of a second as you get a foretaste of the glory to which we look forward.

Just the other night Bishop Julie (another great colleague of mine; I am blessed with good colleagues), and I were being asked a series of questions in a Deanery Meeting in the Diocese. Someone asked us where we felt closest to God?

My answer, almost verbatim, was that ten years ago I could have given you a very predictable answer to that question. I knew the answer to it then. Now, though, my role means that I'm in many different contexts and I'm almost always there to serve (although I keep getting surprised when God hijacks me with love in his eyes and a grin on his face). On the day I was asked the question, though, I had felt closest to him in reading the Scriptures first-thing in the morning as part of my daily pattern of devotion.

Please don't be surprised when God surprises you with his love or overwhelms you with a sense of his goodness.

Equally, don't be too worried when the things which have been life-giving patterns to you begin to feel like they are drying up because the joy-giving things are scooped up into your vocation and become more about service to others than they are about an intimate cuppa with Jesus.

I notice two mistakes we make when that happens: one is to beat ourselves up and assume that we are missing something. "I used to go to X or Y or do Z and feel like I was dancing barefoot with Jesus and could go back and face anything... now I feel like my prayers are bouncing off the wall, and I am sure it is my fault."

Was it Elijah's 'fault' that he found himself alone under a tree in the desert? Maybe it was, maybe it wasn't but this certainly isn't the point of the text.

Don't beat yourself up.

If it's a problem, you can be sure that God is actively seeking to address it. Indeed, you can be sure that God is even more keen to address it than you are. Don't lose the hunger! Don't stop heading to the mountain! And don't be surprised when he meets you in a whole new and unexpected way. He may well have wanted to meet you in another way to teach you more in order that you might be a more effective servant in the first place. He is not in the business of giving up on people.

If the first mistake is beating yourself up, we have just stumbled on the second: don't lose the hunger.

When I was a child, my mum used to pick my sister and me up from school and take us to the ASDA to do the weekly shop. I am sure they would see me coming and start pumping the smell of fresh bread into the store. My main memory of those trips was coming out of school feeling like I hadn't eaten for a fortnight and then smelling that mouth-watering smell. Every single week there was always at least one empty bread packet in the trolley (which mum duly paid for of course).

Don't lose the hunger for Jesus!

Find the places, people, and resources that build your appetite and encourage your desire for holiness and love. Look for whatever is your spiritual equivalent of the smell of baking bread, and regularly hang out around it.

It's not about the formula. It's not about the place. It's not even about the people, the tradition, the habits, or the music. It is about the hunger.

Because all of this depends upon Jesus.

The Methodists have this amazing covenant prayer which they use at the start of each year.

> *I am no longer my own, but thine.*
> *Put me to what thou wilt, rank me with whom thou wilt.*
> *Put me to doing, put me to suffering.*
> *Let me be employed by thee or laid aside for thee,*
> *exalted for thee or brought low for thee.*
> *Let me be full, let me be empty.*
> *Let me have all things, let me have nothing.*
> *I freely and heartily yield all things*
> *to thy pleasure and disposal.*
> *And now, O glorious and blessed God,*
> *Father, Son, and Holy Spirit,*
> *thou art mine, and I am thine. So be it.*
> *And the covenant which I have made on earth,*
> *let it be ratified in heaven. Amen.*[3]

Invitation 7: boldness

It is only now, perhaps, that we can observe that vocation often involves boldness. I think we tend to think this will come sooner, as if vocation really were some kind of action

---

[3] This traditional version is taken from the United Methodist Church Website

adventure movie. All of the prophets who were really prophets in this drama needed to be very bold indeed, but in Elijah we see how that boldness is shaped by the bigger context of a life of obedience, worship, and humility. Godly boldness often doesn't look or feel as we think it will in advance.

Boldness is the willingness to do the right thing even though it is difficult. It is responding to the voice of God even though it might be unpopular.

One of the 'famous facts' about the Bible is that it tells us not to be afraid 365 times and that is 'one for every day of the year'. I often wonder what it means exactly, because I quite often feel fearful in one way or another. I am not an expert but I think that there is a difference between feeling fear and choosing to respond to that fear. (We discussed this earlier with regard to Ahab; see page 82) The question is not really whether something scares me, so much as whether I trust God to be big enough to deal with it.

A word of caution here, though, just because something is bold does not mean that it is Godly! Often it won't be. This section is deliberately brief because the point is a simple one and should not be overplayed. Vocation is tricky and does demand courage. I can't think of an example in the Bible where this is not the case, so don't be surprised when vocation feels hard or demanding: God will have prepared you. He will go with you. He will provide for you, and he will never abandon you.

Invitation 8: imagination

Perhaps the most surprising insight into vocation that this chunk of the Bible brings is the creativity, imagination, and playfulness that we see at work in the prophetic vocation. I suppose I am thinking particularly of Micaiah who is about to bounce onto stage for the dramatic finale, although the overall shape of the narrative suggests this of others too. Whatever you think of his methodology it is very creative, and turns out to be quite effective.

Maybe it is a hangover from our over-equation with 'vocation' being linked to a staid version of ordination and to fairly static careers, but I do think that we get too 'grown up' when we start talking about things like vocation. We can imagine that having a vocation is dreadfully serious with no wriggle-room for personality or warmth.

Anglicans wear robes, traditionally, for many reasons, but one of them is supposed to be that the individual wearing the robes is covered up so that people concentrate on God rather than on us. I kind of get that, but also worry about it (this is not a point about robes). Of course, I am there to serve when I lead worship, and I am certainly there to point people to Christ not to me. The last thing you need is me bouncing around as if I were the centre of the universe. However, if God always wanted a standard approach then he would have designed humanity differently, I think. You don't necessarily want your GP turning up in the surgery dressed as if for a night clubbing, or your child's teacher inventing new spellings just for fun, but the fact that we helpfully conform to expectations at some points doesn't mean that we are always called to do so. Vocation is not a mechanical or automated, it is a living and dynamic and improvised every time it is inhabited; it is to be lived creatively, joyfully, imaginatively, and even playfully.

Invitation 9: partnership – part one

I notice that vocation is rarely a one-person gig either for good or ill. We started reflecting on Ahab looking at his partnership with Jezebel and we shall end our consideration of the prophets looking at theirs. This invitation is another two-parter as there are a couple of closely linked but distinct things to notice here. The first arises out of God's response to Elijah's melt-down in chapter 19. You will recall that one of the things he was instructed to do was to go and anoint Elisha to be his assistant. Since leaving the widow behind he has been alone and this is not good for him. We are told as much right at the get-go of the Bible, in the creation narratives. 'It is not good for man to be alone' (Genesis 2.18). This is a point about humanity not just maleness, lest anyone think otherwise.

As we read the biblical narrative we see the same phenomenon time and again. Moses teams up with Miriam, with Aaron, and later with Joshua. Esther is assisted by Mordechai. Naomi is given the gift of Ruth's loyal companionship. David is strengthened by Jonathan among others. Jesus gathers disciples around him, and when he sends them out he sends them in pairs.

Ministry is only one of many vocations, but it is one I see a lot of in my role. I don't know how true this is for all vocational pathways, but I do often observe that the two great cancers of ministry are loneliness and bitterness. I don't claim for a moment that that's an absolutely accurate diagnosis of the woes of ministry, but I repeatedly observe it, often comment on it, and have yet to be corrected.

We talked about Ahab's problem with bitterness (page 83), let's notice that we have a responsibility to attend to our own loneliness and other internal dynamics. Vocation can look as if it has to be held alone, and there are sometimes bits of most vocations that are lonely, but the weight of any calling is too much for one person to hold alone.

In part, of course, we know that vocation is God's calling and done in God's strength. We partner with him. In every ordination service the ordaining Bishop says to the ordinands 'you cannot bear the weight of this calling in your own strength, pray earnestly for the gift of the Holy Spirit.' Then the Bishop and the candidates, and the whole congregation cry out together 'Come Holy Ghost, our souls inspire, and lighten with celestial fire...' as we wait for his gifts and grace.

In part we recall that we are always invited to partnership in Christ. I am the Bishop of Chester. There is no other

Diocesan Bishop in the Diocese, and the buck stops on my desk. That is weighty and sometimes quite lonely. However, as I look back over this text (and I write this paragraph towards the end of writing the first draft) I find that I have introduced you to many of the people who stand around me. I didn't plan to include them in this way, but noticing that I have I find I am not surprised by it: I could not do this role alone.

You've met Bishops Julie and Sam (who was one of the colleagues who encouraged me to develop this material), my fellow bishops in this diocese. They carry huge loads as well as standing with me, and I with them, as confidantes, friends, prayer-partners, sounding-boards, and co-labourers. Whilst I would not claim all the credit, this partnership is not accidental. I got serious flack online when appointing them when I said:

> *We are looking for two new bishops to join the team and help us 'love Jesus and love others'. We're not looking for heroes, we need people who walk simply and humbly with Christ and inspire others to do the same. We're looking for people who love the church enough to keep us true to our calling. I am looking for colleagues, for me and the rest of my staff team. Will you come and pray with us, laugh with us, open the scriptures with us, dream with us, cry with us, wrestle with us, and share Christian life with us? We want bishops who are as comfortable at a colouring table as they are at the LORD's Table, as ready to don PPE or Wellies as*

vestments, to serve the privileged and the outcast without fear or favour. We want bishops who keep victims central to our safeguarding work, the lost central to our missional work, and Christ central to all that we are.

I simply tried to describe what I was looking for: people who would engage in the episcopal vocation which I lead in this diocese. I think that helped us find what we were looking for, and having found them brings extraordinary life to the diocese and to me personally.

I have also mentioned Lindsay, to whom I am utterly blessed to be married. Her counsel, humour, comfort, challenge, prayerfulness, and company all work together to make the impossible seem less tricky as well as offering balance and perspective in life.

And then there is the office team. I don't know that people understood what I was looking for when we reshaped that team a while ago because the Bishop's office had always simply been a place where work got done. I was looking for a team, that is what we have built, and it transforms the place and my working life. People comment on how amazing Rachel is or how Andy has helped with this or that complex situation (to say nothing of others who are in the team who are also gifts of grace). Neither Rachel nor Andy are the Bishop, but without them the Bishop would probably be in an asylum by now.

Sometimes we will be deployed in teams, and that can be great. Sometimes we won't be. In either situation we need to take responsibility for sharing vocation with others who may be paid or unpaid, near at hand or further away. Vocation is rarely an isolated thing.

Invitation 10: partnership – part two

Finally, though, I want to notice the other great partnership we see in Elijah's life, namely that with the widow of Zarephath. Please don't miss two things here.

Firstly, she was an utter outcast from the perspective of this passage. She is a Gentile. She is a woman. She is a widow. And she is stony broke. She is beyond the covenant. She is female in a very male world. She has no champion or protector. And she has no resources to survive. She doesn't even warrant a name in the text but it is she to whom Elijah is sent. To say that is unlikely is an understatement of the same kind of magnitude as suggesting that folk in Liverpool don't mind football.

Secondly, Elijah is not sent as a beneficent angel of mercy to shower riches. He is sent so that she can put him up and feed him, and in so doing receive amazing provision for the three of them (her, Elijah, and her son). Apparently, there is a Jewish tradition that Elijah hated to trouble people or rely on them, even carrying his own lamp and tapers with him, but here he comes in need and engages in partnership. And it is in this partnership that he is blessed.

This second insight into partnership is vital in many ways, but I separate it to try to protect against the unfortunate thing we can sometimes do when we get the idea that vocation puts us in the 'doing' seat with others in the 'done-to' stalls.

It might be a standard plot line in fiction and a common spiritual fantasy, but Christian vocation rarely follows the standard Hollywood script of: 'Me: hero - you: unfortunate person who is blessed to have me turn up...'. True vocation has a bias towards those who appear to be the least, the lowest, the last, and the lost, and it results in partnership in which the sent discovers they are the greatest recipient.

That, at least, is often my experience and it seems to have been at least part of what Elijah discovered in Zarephath.

Vocation is not only shared, it is a two-way street.

10. PANTO ACT 6:
MICAIAH, THE FALSE PROPHETS,
AND THE FAILED KING
(1 KINGS 22.1-40)

The fanfare sounds for the finale. As we settle back into our seats, the voice of the narrator tells is that there was peace, at least between Aram and Israel, for three years. We are reminded that this is a lesson rooted in historical fact and no mere work of fiction. The final act is royal and is humungous in scale. No longer just one royal court but two, not just one named prophet but 400 unnamed prophets and two named ones (although still only one worth listening to), a massive battle and some gruesome dying. Here we see the failure of kingly vocation infecting not only Israel but attempting to do the same to Judah too.

However, let's not get ahead of ourselves. Scene one is starting, and it is mighty impressive.

Scene 1 (vv1-16)

Here we have two kings, robed in all their splendour (see v10) and surrounded by their retinues. Ahab, King of Israel, speaks ostentatiously to his servants, 'Do you know that Ramoth-Gilead belongs to us, yet we are doing nothing to take it out of the hand of the King of Aram?' (v3) And then he turns to King Jehoshaphat with a swirl of golden robes (and surely Jehoshaphat must jump? Please?) to ask if he will go with him to reclaim it. Jehoshaphat says he will and all is sweetness and light between the kingdoms, until...

... Jehoshaphat demands that before acting they inquire of the LORD.

However, this is new, improved Ahab. He has repented. He gathers not just one prophet, but four hundred prophets and asks them. 'Go up,' they say, 'for the LORD will give it into the hand of the king.' And now we see the problem, or at least Jehoshaphat does. He is not impressed and asks if there is a prophet of the LORD who can be asked? (v7)

Here we see the self-interested repentance of Ahab exposed and outshining even the dazzling splendour of his robes. 'There is still one other by whom we may inquire of the LORD, Micaiah son of Imlah; but I hate him, for he never prophesies anything favourable about me, but only disaster.' (v8) Ahab is not interested in listening, only in getting his way and saving his skin.

Nevertheless, Micaiah is called and walks into this astonishing scene. Here are the kings. Here are their servants and courtiers. Here are 400 prophets. And here is Zedekiah son of Chenaanah who has made himself 'horns of iron' and is busy prancing up and down loudly proclaiming that this is how Ahab will 'gore the Arameans until they are destroyed' (v11) (I might have inserted the prancing, but you get the point).

Scene 2 (vv13-28)

Here comes Micaiah, and it is stage whisper time. The messenger points out that 401 prophets are unanimously affirming King Ahab's desire to go to war (v13), and HAVE YOU SEEN THE SIZE OF THOSE HORNS? (OK, I added that bit too, but again, it fits the absurdity of the moment). Micaiah asserts that, 'as the LORD lives, whatever the LORD says to me, that I will speak.'

So, why on earth does he tell the king to go up and triumph? Look at verse 15! He lies.

Did you see the way he looked at us first? The winding-up motion he made behind the king's back? And now I think of it, why is he dressed as a jester?

You might not have noticed, but the king has. He leaps straight onto his high horse and tumbles straight off the other side as he asks 'how many times must I make you swear to tell me nothing but the truth in the name of the LORD?' (v16) And so Micaiah gives it to him straight. I saw Israel scattered like sheep without a shepherd. Everyone knows that the king of Israel takes after King David and is a shepherd king, but not you, Ahab the faithless, and the LORD is letting your people go home in peace (v17).

'Did I not tell you that he would not prophesy anything favourable about me, but only disaster?' Ahab asks as he regains his feet and brushes himself down (although to be honest he might have been better to stay on the floor in the shadow of his high horse) for Micaiah has only just started.

Here Micaiah can really go to town and the pent-up frustration of the last few chapters seems to come bursting out as if all of the prophets speak at once. You think you are so impressive Mr High-and-Mighty? Let me tell you about the real court that I have just been witnessing. The one that is beyond all this, against which all this pales into the sham and panto that it really is. I saw the LORD, and he was high and lifted up and the train of his robe filled the temple (hang on, that is Isaiah not Micaiah, but it is the same court and Ahab knew of it). There is the LORD, the true King of Israel. He is seated on his throne and the host of heaven is all around him (v19). In that court, oh Ahab you blind and witless fool, this King asks who will entice Ahab that he might go up and fall at Ramoth-gilead. Loads of answers are thrown around (I could tell you a few, oh foolish Ahab, you may recognise them from the mouths of your so-called prophets), but let me tell you the suggestion that was taken up and which even you might recognise. A lying spirit came forth and said he would speak through your prophets. You spotted my so-called lie, but are deaf to all those around you. God has decreed disaster (v23).

Don't forget the end of the last chapter! This is done to bring hope not destruction. Prophecy, in this kind of context, works like shouting out to a child playing in the road: you don't tell them that they are about to be run over in order to make sure they are hit by a bus, but precisely the opposite! You shout in order to persuade them to get to the pavement and weep if they don't make it in time.

However, Ahab is beyond listening. Zedekiah steps in and distracts, accusing Micaiah of being misled by the same lying spirit affecting all the prophets. This is probably the saddest point of the whole drama, and one of the many places we see it is not really, or not only, panto. Ahab and Jehoshaphat will not listen and it's off to war that they go.

Scene 3 (29-40)

Bizarrely enough, even now, Ahab thinks he can outwit God. He seems to think he is cleverer than the Almighty. He heads into battle in civvies having persuaded King Jehoshaphat to go robed as the king, and thus the target. I am not sure Jehoshaphat can have been this much of a dunce in real life, but he walks into this one and is pursued by enemy soldiers (v32). God is not thwarted, though, they see he is not Ahab and turn back, and almost incidentally Ahab is killed by an arrow. He will die as a commoner, the dogs will drink his blood, and the people will be sent home.

And so, the final curtain falls. Ahab is dead. Elijah has gone for now. We hear nothing more of Micaiah ever again. Not all of vocation is on the stage. A strange ending, perhaps, but one that leaves us with much to ponder. This panto is no mere entertainment. It is the well-thumbed banter that can become the foundation of a lifelong conversation about your vocation and the vocation of those whom you have the privilege to serve. Who would you be? How will you follow? What will shape your life? What legacy will you leave?

11. VOCATION OBSERVED: SOME PERSONAL NOTICINGS

That's almost it then, folks, but before we end, I want to do two things for you as we wander home from the theatre and stop to chat before we go our separate ways. One is to ask how you go about discerning vocation in your own life and others, and the other is to make some personal observations about what I see when I look around me in the light of vocational questionings in the church scene in 21st Century Britain.

This comes with no authority beyond what I think I am noticing and I offer it humbly. I start with my observation, though, as these might be some use in your own reflections.

(Human) Problems

Let's start here because there are many problems that we face if we are serious about seeking vocation. Here I don't so much mean theological problems, although they exist as well and we have been addressing some of these throughout this book. I am thinking more of the way that we order ourselves as human society today. I made the point earlier that vocation is given by God but nurtured in the social scene in which we are set (see page 71). This is true on the relational level I was discussing at that point, but it is also true more widely of the context in which we find ourselves.

It is worth noticing some of these human issues which we will encounter in the wider context of our lives as well as when we wrestle with vocation. Observing and naming them will not remove them but it often provides a handle with which we can get at least some kind of grip on them and begin to respond better. Often, it seems to me, we find ourselves needing to negotiate a route that feels like it is surrounded by rocks on one side and perilous things on the other.

Problems caused by abuse

Over the last 25 years it has become clear that we have a huge abuse issue in the Western World. I am aware that putting it like this is a vast understatement, and that this is a beast with many heads and faces. I think particularly, though, of interpersonal and sexual abuse perpetrated against the vulnerable. Sometimes it seems that there is no large institution which has not been complicit in some manner, even if 'only' by staying quiet and protecting its own. Media organisations, educational institutions, medical contexts, children's homes, sporting associations, youth movements, the military, and of course the church have all been tried and found wanting in this regard. IICSA (the Independent Inquiry into Child Sexual Abuse), in its interim report of 2018, quoted the 2015/16 Crime Survey for England and Wales when it notes that 7% of people between the age of 16 and 59 reported having been sexually abused as a child. That means that one in every 14 people report that they have been abused (and given the trauma of reporting such abuse this may well be an underestimate of actual cases). It also means that pretty much every person in the UK will either have suffered abuse or have direct contact with someone who has.

This shapes us deeply, as it should. Abuse is an abomination in any context and must not ever be tolerated.

It is no surprise that we begin to question the institutions that have sheltered abusers and, on occasions, the abuse itself. It doesn't really matter whether their actions were malevolent or naïve, or that society has changed very significantly, there is an entirely understandable breakdown in trust. This naturally raises questions about the place of traditional institutions in our society despite the fact that we are not sure we can do without them.

I have concentrated mostly on God as the one who calls, but I hope I have not ducked the reality that we find vocation shaped in the community of faith, which can be challenging as trust is eroded. The way that God works is usually communal even when he is dealing with an individual. Vocation, in significant part, is discerned together as we have already noted.

Abuse is profoundly sinful, and sin has a way of infecting stuff far beyond itself. Discerning vocation in this context takes care, attention, and patience.

Problems with trust

It is no surprise, then, that we find ourselves with trust issues as a society, but these are even wider than the repercussions of abuse. As I write, Mr Johnson has stood down as British Prime-Minister and when those vying to succeed him were asked on live TV whether they thought him an honest man not one said 'yes' and one simply shook his head (Channel 4, 15th July, 2022: "Live: Britain's Next PM"). On the day I write these words there is controversy reported in the news concerning the former president of the United States, the current President of Russia, and the outgoing President of Sri Lanka.

We often comment that we live in a 'post-truth' world. We feel manipulated by big business, by con-artists pretending they are trying to deliver parcels, by algorithms, and by politicians. We see relationships break down all around us (with somewhere between a half and a third of all marriages ending in divorce).

In this context it would be astonishing if we didn't struggle with trust. My simple observation would be that we flit between struggling to trust at all and trusting too easily. Most of the time we muddle by, sometimes we get hurt, and all too easily we write off those who break our trust without wondering what we might do to address the basic problem.

In a context like vocation, having problems with trust is going to lead to issues. In my role I often meet troubled people who are facing tough stuff. Some, as they come to talk to me seem to be asking me to take away this issue (how I wish I could), but as I pray I find myself wondering whether a significant part of the issue they are facing lies in this area. I think many are wrestling with whether God is really trustworthy, and in that moment I realise I am wondering how to help them trust God more fully. Most of us (including me, incidentally) only trust him a little even when we feel like we are taking a massive step of faith. Things get tricky and we leap back to familiar securities. People come to me as bishop with challenges and often I find that, even if I had a magic wand with the power to make stuff happen, I am not sure what I would try to do with it: their most basic need is finding what God is doing in this particular hard situation and it would not be for me to remove the situation. Most often these are healthy and helpful developmental conversations where tricky issues can be faced and we can engage with the fact that God does need to work through tough stuff with us sometimes. Occasionally it is easier, though, simply to throw the psychological towel in and either walk away or become fatalist: to declare trust broken or assume trust means mindless obedience. Neither is helpful.

God does ask us to trust, and that trust is lived out over the long-haul of discipleship. It is practised, learned, tested, and refined... and it is hard sometimes. However, it is also vital.

Problems around authority

The second thing that is not surprising in a world facing the kind of issues we are exploring here, is that we have something of a problem with authority. Please note what I am saying here as my phraseology could easily be misheard: I am not saying 'you personally are no good at dealing with authority.' You may or may not be, but given that I probably don't know you, and almost certainly don't know you are reading these words right now, how would I know either way? I am saying that we, as a society, have some real issues in this area. If you don't believe me, just think of the shared delight we feel through our media when an authority figure is exposed as being a toerag in one way or another. Where we should grieve, too often we bay and jeer, and this should tell us something.

This is true for society as a whole, at least as represented in our media, I think, and at least a bit true personally as well. If we are honest in our self-examination, we tend to find problems administering authority and problems sitting under it. I don't really like being told what to do, and I don't like telling others what to do, and sadly our view of authority is often quite reductionist in this way. With so few positive role models (at least in terms of authority figures) around, maybe this is not surprising.

Every time a new public ministry begins in the Diocese of Chester the new minister publicly affirms, often standing right in front of me, their obedience.

> *I, A B, do swear by Almighty God that I will pay true and canonical obedience to the Bishop of Chester and his successors in all things lawful and honest: So help me God.*

This takes a bit of getting used to, and to start with I didn't quite know where to look as people were saying the required words. I know that they are swearing obedience to the role not to the person, but it is still strange. However, it is also vital that I exercise that authority, and do so in a Godly, wise, appropriate, and proportional manner. Safeguarding, for example, is not a negotiable option for clergy of this diocese (as, indeed, it is not in any church or diocese). I am under authority, and I am in authority, and I serve no-one by ducking the responsibility of making sure we have done all we possibly can to make our church communities safe spaces for all.

Perhaps it would be healthy if we thought less of power and more of order in these things. A rowing 'eight' (i.e. a boat with 8 rowers like you see in the Oxford/Cambridge boat race each year) is not a hierarchy, but if the rowers want to win they do as their cox says and stay in time with each other. Good order leads to good performance, but it takes real commitment to discover this in wider life.

Much, maybe even most, vocation is ordered, and this is not only the case in the church. If what we do with our lives is simply a job of work we can leave it behind at the end of the day, but if it is vocational it is so more than this. Vocation demands so much more of us in almost every way than simple work, particularly when it comes to engaging with authority, and it also offers so much more. If you are in a profession where the leadership is flawed, how do you engage vocationally in a manner which does not damage you or others? And how do you balance this with God's authority? And how do you exercise your own authority vocationally?

Problems concerning obedience

Here is a third observation in the same area: we have a real problem with obedience (again, I mean this in general terms: there is nothing personal here). I have mentioned this before (see page 104) and I think it is easy to see how it matters for Christians. We want to obey God; as the old hymn puts it, to 'trust and obey, for there's no other way, to be happy in Jesus, but to trust and obey'. However, there are too many troubling stories of obedience being abused within the church.

An early draft of this material was delivered to the Chester Deacons as their 'charge' in 2022. I observed (out loud) that we have so few paradigms for healthy obedience, and turned to look at my chaplain, Andy, who was sitting a few feet away. I asked how the ordinands would feel if I said to him (because he knows me well enough for me to use him as the example in this, I am really leary about playing unconscious power-games with ordinands or others) 'You must obey me!'?

You could feel the discomfort in the room, and I tried to capture and summarise it, observing how that feels like a really dangerous thing to say, not least in our culture. There is a right and proper power dynamic between Bishop and Chaplain that we need to handle well, but demanding obedience could very easily become abusive behaviour.

Yet, at the same time, it is surely true that Andy is there to serve the Bishop in his role as Bishop's Chaplain. I am also there to serve him, of course, and I hope I do, but there is an asymmetric relationship set up by our roles. Today, though, I am not sure we have the necessary framework to think of this as obedience, even in a context like ours, without running into all manner of problems. Children obey teachers, soldiers follow orders, 'my' team does all manner of things for me, be they repeated tasks, specific requests, or matters that they know about long before I ever do. This is not obedience, though, and neither am I suggesting it should be.

In such a context, though, how do we develop a character of obedience before God?

How do we develop language and discover practices that enable us to journey together as disciples in a way that doesn't put any of us in a kind of bullying or unhealthy power relationship? (I am not pretending that I know what the answer to that is, I just notice the problem. Nevertheless, we have to tackle it: one of the very hardest things about being a Bishop is having to call clergy to account. Disciplinary procedures are tough anywhere, but doing them in the church can feel brutal as order appears to clash with grace... but they are vital for the wellbeing of all. I serve no-one if I duck this.)

And so, I ask you the question, how do you learn to practise obedience?

Problems with complaint

Then I notice that we have a real thing about complaint. Some years ago I was doing some chaplaincy with the British Army and we sadly lost one of our soldiers. The BBC reported the loss and got the name of the Regiment wrong (for some regiments you say '67' as 'sixty-seven' and in others as 'six-seven', not that these were the numbers for my Regiment at the time. The Beeb got it the wrong way round, which might not sound much to you but really matters in that context). I was with a group of spouses on camp who reacted with real pain, 'they can't even get the f****** name right!'.

I tried to make contact with the BBC. I searched everywhere for contact details, but the only ones I could find were for the complaints department. I filled in the form, explaining that it was information not really a complaint, but I was the Chaplain et cetera. The name was corrected by the time of the next broadcast.

I was really struck that the only thing I could do was complain, and I really didn't want to. I am grateful for the BBC and they were doing their best. I just wanted to let them know about the error in order to care for my families. Some weeks later I was preaching at our informal service on the second half of Philippians 2. In the NIV verse 14 reads 'Do everything without grumbling or arguing', and the NLT has 'Do everything without complaining and arguing'. In an aside I wondered aloud what would happen if we committed not to complain for a week. The reaction was amazing, and universally negative. It would be impossible, unproductive, and disadvantageous (apparently)...

... the trouble was that I thought I had heard God prompt me, so I agreed with him that I would forgo complaint for a whole week. I set out on some mandatory training the following morning. It was pants. Utter tosh. A complete waste of time. And I could not complain.

The first 24 hours were really tough!

But then I began to notice that I was in a beautiful place, with interesting people, great food, and five whole days to reflect and be. And my week was transformed. Simply by not complaining.

I suspect there are numerous reasons why we have problems with complaint in the Western world, and I am not claiming immunity just because I have glimpsed a better alternative. I have had a few good experiences of not complaining, but I am still afflicted and constantly being reinfected with the disease. Like COVID-19, it appears to have become endemic to Western Culture, and there is little telling concerning the level of impact it will have when it strikes. It's not good for you when you are the complainer, and it is pretty rotten being the complained-at too whether or not you deserve it. I have glimpsed something of the other side, though, where complaint features less and appreciation more, and I find myself pretty certain that the grass really is greener on this other side.

A problem when it comes to individualism

Finally, I think we have real problems with individualism, not least because it is so much part of our culture that we are blind to it. We usually idolise the individual and often neglect the communal in a manner which is starkly obvious when you visit non-western cultures and experience family or village life. I once worked with a curate from an Asian culture who repeatedly tried to help me understand this as we discussed family, and evangelism, and even our team relationships. "You are not a colleague," he said to me one day, "you are my teacher. In my culture a teacher gets so much more respect than you allow me to give you." For us in the West, though, the individual is supreme: my choice, my rights, my potential, my life, my identity, and my wellbeing, all too often outrank 'our' choice / rights / potential / life / identity / wellbeing. This is not selfishness exactly (although it can be), it is more a philosophical and societal framework within which we form our thinking and thus our acting, not least because we are fairly sure this is the way that others will think and act. We had better look after number one, we are told, because no-one else is going to.

We have discussed how such individualism is problematic for discernment. I confess I have chuckled wryly over this as I have sat in socially distanced isolation with COVID-19 writing this uncommissioned book on vocation wondering if there is ever individually discerned vocation. I guess there might be, but am not persuaded, for even here in my disease-ridden study cut off from the world I have been talked into writing this by many others, some of whom I have mentioned.

The problems stemming from individualism are rampant, and I am not sure I add much by writing at length on them here. We see them as we work on deployment, as we seek to develop fellowship, and as we try to grow discipleship to name but three. They warp our understanding of ministry, erode any understanding of religious life, twist our finances, and perpetuate injustice. We really do have an issue here which is challenged directly by the gospel of our LORD Jesus

Christ, but space prevents me rambling too far down this already well-beaten track.

Opportunities

It is natural, perhaps to start with the problems we face, not only because they are demanding, but also because we need to navigate them when we try to discern vocation. However, we also have a great many opportunities when it comes to vocation today. Indeed, each of the problems we note in the previous section is also an opportunity for the gospel to shine a different light on today's world.

There are many more opportunities, although they will vary in specific contexts. It does seem to me, for example, that there is a very common set of hungers in our world today. People long for purpose, for identity, to be part of something that makes a difference. I am sure that we want those things in most generations, but they do seem to stand out at the moment, and they do seem to be a big reason why it is vital that we rediscover our ability to talk about vocation.

Again, though, this section is not intended to be a comprehensive overview of the opportunities we have, more a prompt to think them through. Here are a few thoughts to get the conversation started.

Opportunities to transform the 'secular' week

Even finding a title for this section is hard. What I am suggesting is that discussing vocation begins to open up reflection on how we engage more fully with God throughout the week, and also how we might interact more healthily in the things that we do outside church. So, for example, I suspect that:

- Discussing vocation opens conversation about how we live out our faith throughout the week.
- Discussing vocation rather than work can offer appropriate value to those whose calling is not paid, the retired, the carer, the single parent, the sick, or the housebound.
- Discussing vocation can break the cycle of materialism, unhealthy ambition, and competition which so often dominates high-pressure work places.
- Discussing vocation in a work setting potentially balances the whole of life, for example holding the vocation to be a good husband alongside that of needing to sell 25 motorbikes each day this week (or whatever work target we may have). It brings God into the conversation about the whole of life.
- Discussing vocation asks ethical, moral, and character questions in every place of life that is also a locus of vocation.
- I even wonder whether discussing vocation helps begin to transform our confusion over rights and responsibilities in life. Of course, it can compound

problems if people come to believe that they not only have a particular right without the corresponding responsibility, but that such a right is God-given, but grace has a way of working through such questions in time (especially when we work it though in conversation).

Our lives are, or can be, transformed as we begin to reflect on vocation.

Opportunities to address confusions

There are lots of areas in which we have the opportunity to do further work as a church as well. Again, let me note a few of the things that I think we are a bit confused about or missing:

- I have already confessed that I think we are confused about lay ministry and ordained ministry in the Church of England. At one level I am pragmatic and not sure that this really matters, but at another I fear we miss out on the opportunity to explore what a Holy and Ordered life in Holy Orders could really mean in today's world.

- Alongside this, I do wonder if we need a clearer sense of shorter-term vocation within the church. It is fine to be a teacher for a period, but may not be quite OK to be a priest in the same way. It feels odd to advocate differently, but what do things like *A Year in God's Time* or the Church of England's *Ministry Experience Scheme* teach us about different lengths of calling?

- As I have sought to argue throughout this book, we very much need to develop our thinking about lay vocation beyond the church. Our discussions of vocation are (at best) warped by our fixation on ordained-shaped vocation, and often seriously confused. LICC (the London Institute of Contemporary Christianity) and others are helpful here but they are the beginning of our pondering not the end of it, I think.

Opportunities to meet needs

Similarly, I wonder if a clearer conversation about faithful, relevant, and imaginative vocation would assist us in meeting some of the needs that we clearly see before us. Again, by way of example:

- I have mentioned the regrettable decline of religious communities and my conviction that we should be doing more to address this. Clearly this is only possible as people discover and inhabit that particular vocation. Vocational conversation sparks vocational conversation, I observe.
- A second area of need that may well be enriched in wider conversation around vocation is in the area of spiritual disciplines, habits, or practices. These are not as popular as a topic as they once were, but are essential if we are to follow Christ. They work both ways round, in terms of the big disciplines (like prayer, regular worship, daily study of the scriptures, giving, and so on) which shape our engagement with our vocations, and

the vital micro-disciplines (like offering to make cups of tea or remembering people's birthdays) which shape who we are within it and before God.

- Thirdly, I wonder if this might help us remember what it is to be human as we wrestle with big questions like those around vocation. The world does seem to get busier, more remote, and less personal and people do not thrive in such a context. Engaging the Creator in the midst of our living is not a bad way to reflect on who we are called to be at the heart of our very selves before God.

- Finally, I suspect that clearer conversation about vocation enriches all vocation. It is certainly true that clergy need to be better at discussing all manner of vocational practice with those in their care, but they will be infinitely enriched as they share, vicariously (if you will forgive the pun) in the treasure of what God is doing in and through others' vocation.

So what about you?

I wonder where this all leaves you, then?

I hope that you have had a chuckle, been challenged a bit, encouraged to think, and begun to wonder. However, it is entirely possible that you picked up this book because you think you might have a vocation and you are not sure how to explore it.

Let me offer you a few gifts that might help you explore where you are in terms of your own vocation. I can't tell you what it is, ultimately no-one can, but God will make it clear if you are willing to explore it with him. Here are some tools that might help you from the work that we have done.

A health check

I notice a number of contrasts that come through the text with which we have been living. One exercise you might try is to ask where you would place yourself on a scale between the following terms. This is not some magic internet quiz, but might highlight areas that the Holy Spirit is challenging you. You will also notice that I have not tried to do anything clever with this: don't over think it, just work down the list and see if anything jumps out that you need to work on.

When you think about vocation do you think you are:

Looking at yourself .... Looking at others

Fearful .... Hopeful

Worrying....................................... Trusting

Manipulative .... Open

Disobedient .... Obedient

Hidden .... Transparent

Resentful and sullen .... Emotionally engaged

Jealous.. Creative

Alone .... In fellowship

Dissatisfied .... Joyful

Rushing .... Patient

Serious .... Playful

Harsh .... Kind

Superior.. Alongside

Desperate ....Urgent

If any of these do leap out, why not spend some time exploring why they do, if possible with a trusted friend? Both positive and negative reactions can be really useful as we pray through our vocation. It might not lead directly to an 'answer' but may well place you in a healthy place to explore one.

A reminder not to despise (or idolise) the spiritual

Let me pause and make explicit something that I have been taking for granted. The God who calls, is living, active, involved, and able to speak. I recently had a conversation with an amazing nun from South Africa who told me that she was called to be a sister when God spoke a Zulu word to her in a dream. She did not understand the word as it was a different dialect to her own, but later found it meant 'nun' when she visited a convent with her school. Her calling was confirmed in many different ways alongside this, but she heard the LORD speak to her. My own vocation has been shaped by a few profound spiritual experiences that I cannot explain rationally except by the deep conviction that God can speak. Sometimes vocation does come through a dream, a word, or a direct revelation. Sometimes it is shaped by a part of the liturgy, or a Bible passage that just keeps turning up. Sometimes the same thing just keeps leaping out at you and it feels like God is tapping you persistently or insistently on the shoulder.

Please, though, don't fall into the other two mistakes it is easy to make in this regard (the first mistake being to forget that God does speak like this). Don't try to hold God to ransom to only speak to you in one way. God is God, and will speak to you in his own time, his own way, and in ways that you need to hear him. It is all too easy to miss God's call because we are so keen to hear in exactly the same way as our friend or hero or favourite preacher did. (This is not a bad desire, incidentally, but it is often misplaced. If someone we trust tells us God has spoken in a particular way, it is relatively easy to assume that if God speaks he will do so in the same way because that is how you will know it really is him speaking. The 'trick', though, particularly when it comes to listening to God, is to learn to attend at least as much to the speaker as to what you think is being spoken.)

Secondly, don't think that your experience of hearing God speak is some kind of trump card. Hearing God's voice always needs to be held in deep humility, not least because we are not very good at hearing. When God speaks, he will bring it to fulfilment, but it will often be in ways that you do not expect. I have often sat with people who tell me that 'God has spoken to me and told me I will be ordained.' We have a conversation where I assure them that if God has said that, he will arrange for them to be ordained. However, I gently ask, might we start by agreeing that God has spoken to them and asked them to explore being ordained, so that we can listen and pray together as we seek to understand what is best for them and the church. We explore the reality that our hearing is not always perfect, the deep need to trust that God is utterly able to bring to fulfilment the things he is calling us to, and that proper discernment with others is all part of that Godly process. There is a place of humble trust that accompanies encounter which is essential to our discipleship if it is truly to be authentic. This is what we see in 1 Corinthians 12, I think, as we have already seen.

Different Wisdom

The third gift I want to bring you is quite different. I mentioned that I am writing the main draft of this whilst holed up with COVID-19, during which time my extraordinary daughter Pippa was on a summer placement in a mission hospital in Madagascar. Earlier today as we were texting, the following conversation took place (I reproduce it verbatim less the occasional personal bit, and with permission).

Pippa T
How's writing going?
10:15

Working on what I think is the final chapter, but wondering now if I need another one?
10:16

> Might be a section in the final chapter though
> 10:16

Pippa T
Ahh okay
10:18

Pippa T
What's your extra bit you might need a chapter for?
10:19

> How you go about discerning vocation
> 10:19

Pippa T
Pray
10:19

Pippa T
Conversation
10:21

Pippa T
Oh wait you're answering not asking a question
10:23

Pippa T
Hahah sorry
10:23

> Not at all – keep them coming...
> 10:25

Pippa T
Observing yourself
10:25

Pippa T
Both what you enjoy
10:26

Pippa T
And what you are good at
10:26

Pippa T
And what causes you to grow
10:26

> (I am pasting these directly into the text... although might edit later)
> 10:27

Pippa T
And looking at different vocations together e.g. being an air hostess probably doesn't fit in with a calling to get alongside and mentor young people 10:27

Pippa T
Or an astronaut 10:28

Pippa T
What energises you 10:28

Pippa T
The ways you can give and feed and encourage each other 10:28

Pippa T
Read God's word obvs 10:30

Pippa T
Discerning what you enjoy, good at, grows you etc are all determined in conversation with Godly friends/leaders /those around you, and prayer, and reflection alone, and being stuck in God's word 10:30

Pippa T
Something about knowing boundaries and temptations and what's healthy for you 10:33

> You could be writing this book you know
> 10:37

Pippa T
For someone who grew up in a spiritualist culture, being a yoga instructor may be unwise 10:41

> Pippa T
> **But being a yoga instructor isn't unGodly in and of itself**   10:41

I don't need to say more as the conversation speaks for itself, partly because there is some great content, but partly because we get to talk and in talking, with Christ at the centre, wisdom is so often found.

Questions

The final gift I can think to offer you is a series of questions upon which you might like to reflect if you are wrestling with your own vocation. Again, these are not exhaustive, authoritative, or final. They may, though, be useful.

Some questions around your own observations:

1) When do you feel closest to God and most alive?
2) Which characters or stories in the Bible leap out most clearly to you? How might you set aside a little time to 'live more intentionally' with these characters or events to help you notice what you notice and pray it through?
3) What thoughts refuse to leave you when you are praying or worshipping?
4) Do you have recurring dreams, thoughts, words, or pictures which seem significant as you pray?
5) Who do you most admire in life? Could you take some time, and perhaps some space in your journal if you keep one, to explore what it is that you admire and where within that admiration there might be something of God's call? (It is worth noting that Ahab's example

also makes the shadow side of this question potentially valuable, for example asking about things that always make you fume).

6) What would you most like people to say about you at your funeral?

Some questions about what others see and say:

1) What do others most value in you?
2) Are there any themes that keep returning in what Godly friends tell you that you should be doing with your life?
3) Where do you see fruit around you in your discipleship?
4) What are the most uncomfortable things people say about you?
5) What would your closest friends describe your priorities as being?

Some questions about choices you make:

1) With whom do you ally yourself?
2) To whom do you listen, and how do you attend to listening well?
3) More than that, who do you allow to speak truth into your life, into your innermost places?
4) Or, to ask a similar question in a different way, how do you judge who might be sage or prophet in your life?
5) And how will you make space for the uncomfortable people who speak God's truth to you?
6) And how do you make space to learn from the 'utter numpty' moments (see page 118)?

7) Where and how do you embrace your playful side (see page 119)?

8) How do you filter out the siren calls that would lead you astray, for example popularity, power, achievement, or possessions?

Some questions about your priorities

1) To what extent is your exploration of vocation about a living relationship with Christ in practical ways in your daily life?

2) How are you making space for him to change your life in the way that you pray he would change others?

3) What micro-disciplines (see page 118) do you adopt (or should you adopt) to foster your character in Christ as you explore vocation?

Conclusion and Prayer

So, three very simple thoughts as we say our goodbyes:

Vocation is about learning to trust. It is a life-long and daily wrestle with how we do obedience to God, and faithfulness to those we serve. It's about how we learn the secret of contentment. It's about learning to trust.

Secondly, our vocation is to work really hard at loving people and loving God. It's listening hard, it's laughing easily. It's about not taking ourselves too seriously or thinking of ourselves too highly. It's about striving to be nothing but honest and straightforward in the ministry that we inhabit.

And, vitally, our vocation is about delighting in Jesus. Again: translate that into language that works for you in your own context, because the exact words aren't magic or formulaic, but it really is around delighting in Jesus. It's about drinking deep at the fountain of his word. It's about regularly wasting time in his presence. It's about ensuring that nothing but nothing is more important than that central and core relationship in your life. In so doing discover you will discover the utter joy and glorious liberty of participating in God's own work and find life in all its fulness for yourself and others.

> *I am no longer my own, but thine.*
> *Put me to what thou wilt, rank me with whom thou wilt.*
> *Put me to doing, put me to suffering.*
> *Let me be employed by thee or laid aside for thee,*
> *exalted for thee or brought low for thee.*
> *Let me be full, let me be empty.*
> *Let me have all things, let me have nothing.*
> *I freely and heartily yield all things*
> *to thy pleasure and disposal.*
> *And now, O glorious and blessed God,*
> *Father, Son, and Holy Spirit,*
> *thou art mine, and I am thine. So be it.*
> *And the covenant which I have made on earth,*
> *let it be ratified in heaven. Amen.*[4]

---

[4] This traditional version is from the United Methodist Church Website

12. Postscript

(over coffee a week later)

———————————————————

Vocation is not a theoretical thing. It is lived, often messy, and it is worked out in the real lives of real people. One of the things I love most about my own vocation is listening to others as they explore theirs. So, imagine we have met for coffee a week or so after the panto and begin to hear each other's own experiences of vocation. This is the conversation with which I want to leave you before we finish: I am really not interested in just writing an interesting book or offering a new idea: the reason I have written is with the little hope that God may do massive things in you and this conversation may be a small part of that. There is a dying world in desperate need of Jesus' gift of hope, forgiveness, and reconciliation, and God is recruiting team members from and for every walk of life.

Various folk have agreed to share something of their own journey with you, and I share these cuttings from our shared scrapbook of vocation with the hope that you will spot something of yourself in one or more of my friends. (There are three examples here, I plan to have others available on the website as well. The link to this is at the back of this book along with a QR code.)

All of these stories are unfinished (as is mine, and yours), and I am really grateful to everyone who has been willing to share their experience. If they are half as much of a blessing to you as each of them is to me then I can think of few better ways to end this book.

Meet Bernie

My name's Bernie and I have always ended up with jobs where I could help people in practical ways to achieve their goals. I was not a Christian until I was 38, so my life before this was not directly shaped by me trying to follow God. I didn't make all the decisions myself, exactly, if things felt natural I believed they were right.

I grew up on a small-holding miles from the sea and always wanted to experience something different in life. I was the adventurous one in my family, I suppose, and I ended up serving in the Navy for 22 years, but it wasn't a direct 'I am going to join the navy', really. I had wanted to join the services at 18, but my dad had put me off.

When I was 21 I went into Lincoln and walked down the street with all the recruiting offices on it. The Navy one was the first one I found. That was how I came to be in the Navy; I just wanted to experience a bit more of life and worldwide places.

When I first joined it was just a job, sort of, but it became more than this once I had finished my training. It was enjoyable, learning things I knew nothing about; I became an aircraft engineer and the Navy became more than a job, it was a life.

I was still in the Navy when I became a Christian, through the Naval Christian Fellowship in Portland with Padre Ray Jones. I think that being a Christian did make a difference to the way I was at work. It introduced me to like-minded Christians that I didn't know existed, and made me more tolerant of people who would have irritated me before, and less tolerant of bad language.

When I left the Navy I did a bit of work as a Home-Help and also trained as a driving instructor. The thing that drew me to driving instructing was working with people and helping them to achieve their goals. The same sort of thing with Home-Help, really, I was supporting people in need.

The thing was, though, that I didn't like sitting in the car all day as a driving instructor. I am more of an active person than that, so when I was sat in church one day and saw an advert for a caretaker job, my wife and I prayed about it and we decided that I would take on the job. I loved that job. I was serving God and meeting lots of people I could encourage and serve in practical ways. I helped them and saw God at work and good things happening and that was very satisfying.

I haven't thought that much about it being a vocation, but I believe God has put me in places where I have been able to help people and make a difference to their lives. He was guiding me before I knew He was. It is not so much that God has ever said to me 'do this' or 'do that', but I have found God where I am; there are lots of things within His plan for my life, I'm sure. Sometimes we want God to take control, but He gives us a choice and meets us there.

The advice I would give to a new Christian in terms of finding God's plan or purpose for your life is to follow your passions (so long as they are not illegal!) and be willing to test things out. You will often find that you are good at things you had no idea you would be good at. God may not reveal the whole future to you. And pray, of course, and by following God's Holy Spirit, who is within you.

I now know it is that feeling of right and wrong, reflecting how God is leading us by His Holy Spirit and it is all about knowing God and the life that He wants us to live. This means you begin to feel uncomfortable if you start to stray from what He wants.

In terms of mistakes: be careful of being drawn into the wrong kind of company. Sometimes you know it is the wrong company, but you still go there and then you end up doing things that you don't really want to do.

I am a practical person more than a head person. God needs all sorts of people to serve him and I am glad He uses me and my gifts.

Meet Rachel

Hello hello! I'm Rachel (the Rachel you have already read about, except an altogether less polished version from my perspective).

When I was growing up, I always loved meeting up with family members and old friends, but used to dread the inevitable question "So, what next?". Will you go to University? What will you study? What then? What next? I never knew. My A-Levels were a 50:50 split Arts and Sciences (I wanted to keep my options open) and I picked a degree at Uni that would allow me to study three subjects concurrently (our course hoodies had a slogan on the back which read 'Indecision is a decision too'). I have never known what I want to be 'when I grow up' (other than a Blue Peter presenter, but then who doesn't want to be one?).

When people asked, I would have loved to have been able to say, 'I'm going to Uni to study Medicine so I can be a doctor' – but for some reason I didn't feel I could commit to pursuing such a career, so the answer instead was always 'I'm not really sure'. As I reflect back on that period now, I can see that although I may have felt adrift and unsettled (or occasionally panicked) because I didn't 'have a plan', the time was characterised more by a contented peacefulness (except when I could see someone with a 'and after that…?' tripping off their tongue. Panic ensues). Now, I think I can I attribute the peacefulness to my learning to trust God; that He would point me in the right direction, clearly leading the way to whatever was right.

Maybe what has felt to me like indecision has allowed God to direct my vocation (vocation being a word I had only really associated with vicars or the vocational career paths I was always so wary of...). I look back on what seemed to be entirely random and coincidental job offers and realise how I 'just happened' to be in the right place at the right time. I can see how I had been growing, learning, and gaining experience in each role, all of which would lead me to where I am now. God had prepared the way entirely without me realising and I'm convinced the journey itself (with its bizarre mix of peace and panic) has been an important part of my vocation. Most recently, He prodded me to apply for a job I felt entirely unqualified for (and He seemed to nudge those who appointed me to take a chance on an enthusiastic but inexperienced newbie too). Is this my 'vocation'? Not fully I don't think (job and vocation are not quite the same thing), but it is definitely part of it.

I know I am in the right place and I am ridiculously happy in this role, but even here I would be giving a dishonest and unhelpful picture if I pretended it was all simple and straightforward. Sometimes I wonder if people really value the work I do or see me as 'only' an administrator. I can find myself thinking that I am the least important person in the room (even when others seem to value me) because that is the stereotype associated with the role. I am no stranger to imposter syndrome (when others describe their imposter syndrome I even manage to wonder if I am an imposter in the imposter syndrome club). Following Jesus vocationally doesn't stop these inner doubts or unhelpful views, but it does give me somewhere to take them.

Amazingly though, more often I am blown away by how remarkable it is that I love my role as much as I do. I have genuinely never woken up and dreaded going to work (I understand from friends that this is rather exceptional). For me, part of embracing vocation has been about turning away from judgements and expectations (of my own and the world) and stepping into the place that God has mapped out; where I feel at home when I sit down at my desk, where I find myself laughing often and easily, and where I challenge myself to do better every day out of a love for the team, the role and the way it enables me to serve God and His church. I have been abundantly blessed to learn that work sometimes (if you're really lucky, often) doesn't feel like work at all.

Now, if I ever find myself speaking to a young person or new Christian thinking about their vocation, I make a conscious effort to try and have a helpful and encouraging conversation, rather than one that feels like a test. It can't just be me whose toes used to curl at the 'So, what next?' question (and I always thought it was dreadfully unfair that grown-ups could ask that of me, but it would seem impertinent for me to ask it back...). I hope that asking about their strengths, gifts and what brings joy will be a far more enjoyable (and, I'm sure, beneficial) conversation for all involved.

I still don't really know what I want to be when I grow up, but I'm confident that I can trust the God who knows me better than I know myself to point me in the right direction. Right now, that is here. I might, or might not, still doing this job in 20 years' time, but I am sure I will look back and see how this has been part of a vocational journey which is far bigger than any one task, time, or role.

And if God ever nudges me towards a Blue Peter application form, the pen will be ready...

Meet Reb

My name is Reb, I am 23, and I spend most of my time working as a Research Assistant in a university laboratory. I really enjoy my work, which comes from a fascination with the intricacies of life and the freedom of creativity and innovation that scientists have to try new experiments and discover new things. By training, I am a scientist. It began when I was at school; a crazy science teacher helped me to work out that I could do and love Biology and Chemistry. I love to learn, a value that has been instilled by and grown alongside watching the way my parents do life, so it makes sense that I should enjoy a career where learning is never over.

Since finishing a degree in Biology, I have worked in amazing labs doing really cool frontline science. Every day, I am surrounded by incredibly talented people whose brains can both store an inordinate amount of information and churn out imaginative idea after idea. It is daunting and an absolute honour to be surrounded by all of these people. However, I keep finding that I don't quite fit in. I am frequently confronted with thoughts that question my legitimacy as a scientist, my lack of drive to work all hours of the day towards a discovery, and my failings as I try to embrace an intellect-focussed career with my people-minded personality.

Do you know what I love? Making people cups of coffee. I love the look on their faces when they realise you've remembered how they like it and made it for them at the time of day when they like it. I love smiling and saying hello to people as I walk around the building. The more I think about it, the more things I find that set my heart alight. Inviting lots of people over for a meal and discussing the difficult things in life, crying and laughing together. Going round to friends who are struggling with the capacity to do life's menial tasks and cooking for them and folding their laundry. Inviting a refugee to stay in my home. Caring for children who believe themselves unwanted. In my perfect life, I have time for everyone who needs someone, always have the kettle boiling and always have a spare bed for someone who needs it. Maybe I am a pastor? Or a pastoral figure? I wonder if that is my vocation.

In practice, this is not what my life looks like. For most of my week, I work. I intersperse it with church commitments, running, and visiting friends and family. Sometimes this is really quite dissatisfying. On other days, I remember that my vocation is not limited to a space or occupation; being available for my colleagues may sometimes be where God wants me more than anywhere else. The beautiful thing about my vocation is that it is valuable everywhere. What makes it hard is that it is really difficult to be everyone's person all at once, especially with a full-time job and all the rest.

I was challenged by Mark's contrasts (page 157) and realised that I have a lot to learn on the 'Rushing' v 'Patient' axis. I think I love that vocation is a lifelong lesson. Maybe one day I will be pastor-ing full-time, or maybe I will find a way to host and love people without rushing around like a headless mother hen. I trust that God refines us as we lean into him, which is why listening to his voice on vocation is so important. Ultimately, vocation all points back to him.

To those wondering about vocation, I would encourage spending time over the questions on the previous pages, really meditating on them and not allowing time pressure to become a burden. It is a wonderful journey realising the things that both lighten your soul and terrify you, noticing as you do the ways God has been changing your heart as you have walked with him. I am blessed to call Mark and Lindsay godparents, and have discussed many of these thoughts and worries with them in the last few years. Finding life-giving folk who root for you in all seasons is a rarity but often breeds the most beautiful discourse. Vocation wonder-ers would do well to plough energy into identifying and investing in such people.

A pastoral scientist – not what I expected as a young 15-year-old expecting all the world to be her oyster. An unfinished story this most certainly is, but what a blessing it is to trust all that God still has in store.